Always Thinking of You in Macclesfield

For SHEILA

*who shared many of these
adventures, and has heard
the rest described
time . . .*

after time . . .

after time

Frontispiece: *card sent by one Maxonian to another in the twenties*

GOLDEN DAYS

A Macclesfield Life

Paul Maybury

Copyright © P Maybury, 1995

Published by Sigma Leisure – an imprint of
Sigma Press, 1 South Oak Lane, Wilmslow, Cheshire SK9 6AR, England.

British Library Cataloguing in Publication Data
A CIP record for this book is available from the British Library.

ISBN: 1-85058-553-9

Typesetting and Design by: Sigma Press, Wilmslow, Cheshire.

Cover Design: MFP Design & Print

Cover photograph: Chris Rushton

Printed by: MFP Design & Print

Preface

This Way To Macclesfield

This is a book of Macclesfield memories which I hope may recall times of happiness (and some not so joyous) to those who have shared these years with me.

It is, however, a little more than that, since it attempts to show how a town and its people mould each other. In a most substantial way, Macclesfield with its surroundings and its way of going about things has guided my life; it would not have been the same had I lived anywhere else. In turn, in an infinitesimally small way as chronicled in these pages, I am bound like everyone else to have had some effect, here and there and now and then, on the town.

It follows from this that the memories are mostly mine. People who shared particular events with me will remember them in different ways, but to the best of my belief I have set things down as they actually happened, and I have not deliberately invented anything. Where there are mistakes, therefore, they too are mine, and I apologise in advance for them.

I have been helped – and for this I am grateful – by the recollections and the memory-jogging of my wife Sheila, my elder brother Philip and other members of the family present and past. I have received help also from friends, especially from members of the congregations of the churches at which I have served, and I thank them. I also thank other good friends whom, I fear, I have badgered for the loan of pictures. Finally, I am grateful to the staff at Macclesfield's spanking new library for their help in answering particular queries.

I hope I may have your company as we read on through the years ...

Paul Maybury

Contents

1

Golden Threads, Golden Times

Fairly late in life, when my journalist's job at the *Daily Mail* had been swept away in the rush of computer technology, I took the opportunity to heed an insistent whisper over many years and attempt to enter the church. The selection process for would-be priests is protracted and precarious. Candidates face many interviews with some understandably searching questions. One put to me asked how I would describe my youth, and I replied: 'Golden'.

It was, perhaps, not the most tactful answer. The more I tried to explain it, the more I expanded on the happy years I remembered, the more deeply I felt I was getting into difficulty. When I thought about it afterwards I realised why I had such a sticky interview. The church is more likely to welcome and to favour those who know they have faced problems and overcome them, rather than those who claim not to have had difficulties at all.

And yet, I still do not think I could have answered the question more accurately. The fact is that from my earliest recollections I have been well content with my lot – a sentiment that might become tiresome by its repetition in the following pages. I know myself to be very fortunate, and this state of affairs in my early life I owe to two main influences – my family and my town. My debt to the former will be evident to anyone who reads on to the end, although I shy away from expressing it too fulsomely. But I can try to explain what I owe to the town, because the town can't blush.

Well then, Macclesfield has always delighted me. To the east it is watched over by Shutlingsloe, much as the Theban Peak guards the Valley of the Kings at Luxor in Egypt. Since it is the hills that are everlasting, and they are there whenever we lift up our eyes, we draw from them a rugged and assuring sense of permanence.

Then to the west the hills fall away to the Cheshire plain, whose flower-clad villages offer a promise of gentleness and repose. Add to these scenes the sense of adventure given by the canal and the Bollin and here and there a little lake, and it seems to me you have the best of all possible worlds. As a boy I wished also that we had the sea, perhaps round about Congleton Road, but I suppose that would have been greedy.

However, it is the life of the town, always changing in detail but constant in interest and purpose, the life acted out upon this network of streets and against this background of hills and pastures, that has bound me heart and soul to the place. Charlotte Bronte spoke in one of her poems of a 'web of

childhood, a web of sunny air', and that is what I feel was woven around me
and Macclesfield so that wherever I might go we are inseparable.

The web was woven with especial intensity through the happy chance that
gave me a grandfather who was editor of the *Macclesfield Times*. From earliest
days I was used to the unfolding history of the town running through our living
room. The activities of its organisations, the decisions of its councillors, the
probity or otherwise of a leading citizen all hung in the air about us. I would
not like you to think that they were openly and deliberately discussed in front
of 'the boys', as my brother and I were always known. But I suppose we
absorbed them by a form of osmosis. For one thing, every word that is to be
printed in a newspaper should ideally be read in proof by the editor. In the case
of the *Macclesfield Times*, they were read at our dining room table on two or
three nights every week. We were therefore surrounded by the very tissue of
the town's affairs.

LARGEST GUARANTEED NET CIRCULATION

ⅅacclesfielⅾ Ⅽimes
Congleton Cimes & East Cheshire Observer
(ROTARY PRINTED.)
ESTABLISHED 1872
(Price · Two Pence.)

PROPRIETORS
MACCLESFIELD TIMES LTD.

TELEPHONE No 2070

– THE LEADING LOCAL PAPERS

QUEEN VICTORIA STREET, MACCLESFIELD.

1st April. 1931.

My grandfather had to work hard to reach his position on the paper. We thought
it a high position indeed, and credited him with an importance which in truth
he did not possess. I recall vividly that once in Dr Clegg's waiting room in
Roe Street I was leafing in my childish way through a copy of Picture Post
when I came across an illustrated feature on the staff of **The** Times. I perused
it carefully, and wondered for a long time why my grandfather's face was not
among those pictured. But he was important to us and, I believe he was a great
influence also in an admittedly small town.

Alfred Hanson was a Yorkshire lad from a Gomersal family. When he left
school he was apprenticed first to a printer, at a time when, in most local firms,
everything that had to be printed was set by hand. This involved each letter
being picked up separately from its slot in a wooden case (and put back
afterwards), lined up in a composing 'stick' and spaced out to make one
complete if sometimes wobbly line. This was before the invention of a
typesetting machine which cast the line as one, complete with even spaces.
You can test the effect for yourself in old books – if the spaces in a line are
unequal, and the words tend to go up hill and down dale a bit, then it is handset.

Setting pages in this primitive fashion was intensive work, needing long
training, but it offered the competent man a reasonably rewarding and secure

job (until computers came along). However, my grandfather aimed a little bit higher: he wanted not just to set the words of a newspaper, but to write them. He therefore began by learning shorthand – one of his Sunday School prizes which I treasure is a New Testament printed entirely in Pitman's shorthand.

Thus equipped with the basic skill of a reporter he became an 'articled journalistic pupil', as it was called, on the *Dewsbury Reporter*. Once started he wanted to continue going up. So he sallied forth on his new career taking jobs on a succession of weekly newspapers up and down the country. Each step added to his experience, and each town had its own particular challenge. At Dover he had to set sail in a fishing boat to report on the endeavours of Channel swimmers. At Chelmsford, much more gruesomely, he had to attend at least two executions in the local prison. He would never talk about that, beyond telling my grandmother that he couldn't face his breakfast afterwards.

Letter from the sheriff – passport to witness an execution at Chelmsford Prison

By the time he fetched up at Macclesfield in 1915 with a job as sub-editor and chief reporter on the *Times* he had acquired a wife and two daughters, and they lived at first in Peter Street. At that time the paper was printed by the firm of Heaths in St George's Street, and produced by the simplest of available processes, a flat-bed machine. In this system the type for each page, locked tightly inside a metal frame, is then laid on the flat bed of a printing press. Separate sheets of paper are fed in, and the image of the type is impressed on them by a roller. It is basic and cheap, but it is slow, and worse still, each printed page has to be folded by hand or by a separate machine.

By the time a paper prints 7000 or 8000 copies a week, it needs something faster, and 50 or 60 years ago it had two choices. It could go to the top and buy a rotary press as operated by the biggest papers. This uses a continuous web of newsprint, which is passed at great speed between a roller and a revolving page of type, then automatically cut and folded. The snag, as you will divine, is that the flat page of type has to be converted into a semi-circular printing plate which can be bolted on to a roller, and this is done by taking a mould and casting it in hot lead. This requires more machinery and more skill.

As my grandfather took control he first sought to modernise the paper by installing such a rotary press – bought second-hand – in a new printing works halfway down Churchwallgate. This was a noble venture but, as I was told by one of its survivors, it took time to get the machine right, and several issues contained pictures which looked as if they had been taken in a coalhole. Something better was still needed.

It came with the installation of a Cossar, a prince among local newspaper presses, and this was my grandfather's greatest technological contribution to the *Times*. This machine had the advantage of using a continuous reel of newsprint, but its ingenious design allowed each two-or-three-foot section of it to hover briefly over the flat pages of type while a massive roller snuck up on it and smacked it into contact with the printing surface. This gave it in operation a characteristic and fearsome VROOM-bam-bam roar which could rattle windows for some distance around. There can have been no sleep on press night for the residents of the Castle Inn next door.

The Cossar combined the best of both worlds – flat type, yet continuous newsprint, and in addition the stream of paper passed after printing over yet more rollers which enabled it to be cut and folded without a hand being laid on it.

The ground-floor room housing the machine, together with an upper floor containing further exciting pieces of machinery and equipment, became my boyish playground for as long as I could get away with it. By this time Linotypes – the amazing invention in 1884 of Mr Ottmar Mergenthaler in the US – were standard typesetting equipment, and we had no fewer than five of the beasts. They were a triumph of the improbable, machines made up of clanking cogs and flapping arms, a pot of molten lead and dozens of brass moulds. All this enabled the operator, sitting at a giant keyboard, to assemble a line of moulds, space it automatically to the required width, inject lead against the moulds (which were then returned automatically to their storage magazine) and end up with a slug of lead with a row of letters on the top ready for printing. Hence, a Line o' Type.

Mr Alfred Hanson, left, presents a Macclesfield Times trophy on the bowling green at South Park

Of course, I soon discovered that if the operators – led by Ernest Hackney – could set columns of type for the paper, they could also set the name of the grandson of the paper's editor-manager, and generally they were quite willing to do so. I therefore amassed many souvenirs, and they wasted their valuable hours. It never occurred to me that the staff, and especially Sam Davenport, the works manager, might regard me as a confounded nuisance. They never said so, and they joined in my juvenile endeavours. They worked the perforating machine for me so that I could convert sheets of gummed paper into stamps, they guillotined pads of scrap paper, and a lady named Ethel Brindley helped to 'stitch' my little books with the stapler. It was all great fun.

However, as I got older I discovered there was a line beyond which, quite rightly, they would not go. I might have had my place, but they knew theirs and I could not presume upon it. In my teens, and by then a junior reporter on the paper, I was not to be indulged as I once had been, and really this was for my own good. One press night I was idly wandering alone around the precious Cossar – the machine supremo, Ernie Baker, was presumably next door in the Castle taking refreshment before his long night's work. As I wandered I saw that the little hoist from upstairs had delivered another page of type to be put on the machine ready for printing. I thought: "I'll get that out ready for them". I had actually laid hands on the metal frame when I heard a warning shout from upstairs. One of the printers, guarding his handiwork, had been peering

How things used to be:
members of St George's Mothers' Union tour
the Daily Mail office in Manchester during its
last days of the traditional hot metal printing.
Left: the metal type is locked into a page frame.
Below: the fantastical Linotype machine used
to set the lead 'slugs' of type.

down the liftshaft to see what I was up to, and he told me with no possibility of contradiction not to touch it.

I thought he was being fussy, but I realised later that he was saving me, as well as the paper, from a fate worse than death. As I have said, all the bits of type assembled for a page were locked into a frame and held there only by sideways pressure. If I had moved that frame inexpertly the whole page, about 18 inches by two feet, could have become 'pied' – collapsed into hundreds of separate bits which could never have been reassembled in time for printing that night. I still go cold at the thought of the damage I might have done.

Anyone looking today at the affairs of the *Macclesfield Times* would, I think, be amazed at the wafer-thin finances. We are used now to large newspaper companies spending great sums, even on local papers, with modern offices and adequate staffs and, of course, computers. Such largesse did not exist in days gone by. I see from the accounts of the *Macclesfield Times* company in 1946 that receipts from sales, advertising and printing totalled £21,068 for the entire year, and the profit was £9,257 – which was not a bad return at any rate. Dividends paid to shareholders were £1,747, and I see elsewhere the proud statement that 'we have paid our shareholders consistently a ten per cent dividend and a ten per cent bonus for several years'.

On the expenditure side the largest item naturally covered wages and salaries – £7,296 for the year. But at that time, with staff returning from the war, there must have been at least five editorial staff (we shall meet them later), three advertising and commercial staff, and around 15 printers, an average of only £300 each. But that was quite adequate to keep the operation ticking over nicely.

This was just about the time when the firm took the plunge and at last bought a van, a second-hand blue Morris 5cwt of indeterminate age. Before then the week's supplies of newspapers were delivered to shops in the neighbourhood by taxi, a rather unflattering image for a paper now selling about 13,000 copies a week. I see that running the van – petrol, oil, repairs etc – cost £61.0s.1d, or only just over £1 a week.

The big cheese in the organisation through my years of childhood was Mr Harold W Whiston, a scion of the Whiston silk family which, merged with the vast Brocklehurst enterprise, became BWA, perhaps the biggest set of initials in the Macclesfield silk industry. He was one of seven directors of that firm, but of the *Macclesfield Times* he was the promoter of the company in 1913, chairman and managing director. On the rare occasions when he proposed himself for a visit to our house, to discuss the paper's affairs, there was an air of panic. Philip and I were bundled off to bed out of the way. I do not think we ever saw the great man, except at a distance.

But I do remember viewing some of his gifts, which alas meant absolutely nothing to me at the time. One of these was a woven silk picture of a York airliner, a batch of which was ordered from BWA. For some reason, it seems, the order fell through and BWA made use of them by sticking a calendar on the bottom and giving them to staff, customers and business associates as a goodwill gesture. As calendars, of course, many were casually thrown away at the end of the year. You will not need me to remind you that those pictures of airliners which remain now sell at auction for more than £1000, the most valuable of all the series of 20 or more silk pictures which BWA produced.

Towards the end, and for some reason which I never heard explained, Mr Whiston departed from the scene and my grandfather, successively editor, director and general manager, also took over the chairmanship, retaining it for a short time before in 1946 the paper became part of the Kemsley organisation.

He finished, therefore, at the top of his own particular tree. He got there, as was the custom, with few material aids to success save his native wit and a great skill at shorthand – for many years he acted as official shorthand writer for the Macclesfield bankruptcy courts. He was paid, I remember, by the word and all the thousands of them had to be counted up by hand.

It wasn't until two or three years before retirement that he actually had a typewriter he could call his own. But he longed for one and, since this was wartime and they were scarce, he had to keep an eye open for a second-hand machine. It was delivered, I remember, in the dark of the night when Philip and I had gone to bed. But we heard its tapping, and we got up and opened the door to see this treasure. I shall never forget the beaming face of my grandfather as he pecked at the keys of an ancient Barlock, an ambition realised.

Poor chap, he did not have sole use of his acquisition for long. Every member of the family – down to the youngest, as you see – wanted to be tapping away writing something. Well well, I suppose that was his greatest gift to us.

2

How Much is that Dinky in the Window?

It is not to be expected that a growing lad with an active body and a mind awash with intriguing schemes should evince any interest whatever in what you might call the humdrum type of shops. You know, the establishments selling everyday but unexciting articles like groceries and clothes. Not even Marks and Spencer, whose green-fasciad store in Mill Street was then at the top of Backwallgate, could hold any great attraction, though boys were from time to time dared to go in and peer at the corsets.

No no, the shops that interested me and my peers were of quite different types. First – and we will get this over right away since it might put you off – were the Aladdin's cave kind of shops, full of mystery and promise and, to be honest, smells. The kind of shop where you could poke around happily in the dusty gloom without knowing what you were looking for, and have a sympathetic pair of ears listening to help you find it.

My favourite, I think, was the bicycle-cum-electrics store kept by Mr Bert Mellor at the bottom of Churchwallgate. There could be anything in stock from bicycle dynamos to football adaptors. I remember one day having a long and serious discussion with Mr Mellor about the best type of electric motor to install on my push-bike to give it added zip. You see, I was fifty years ahead of Clive Sinclair the inventor. But Mr Mellor could not oblige with the necessary hardware.

Stanley Street also boasted a treasure-trove shop, which mainly sold rope but many other things besides. I didn't go there too often because of the crotchety nature of the old gent in charge. He once rebuked me for being flippant with him, though I wasn't sure what he meant. I was so nervous that to placate him I bought for sixpence a carrier bag containing two dozen pieces of painted tin which, he assured me, could be assembled into a roller-coaster complete with a little line of carriages. I could see what he meant, but I never could put it together. That taught me not to be flippant.

Another little spot to keep an eye on was the parlour window of a shop in Chester Road, where the do-it-yourself store now stands, and this was used to display any amount of rubbish with boy appeal. I once acquired here a pair of earphones (there goes another sixpence).

These were needed because, like half my class, I was trying to keep up with

the wireless craze, still an amazing mystery to us. How incredible that, out of three or four curious pieces of apparatus, screwed to a wooden board and linked by wire, a voice or music could actually be conjured!

Truth to tell, the most exciting part of the whole project was the need to shin up a drainpipe at home so I could attach the necessary 30ft of aerial wire to the roof. That having been accomplished, I needed a radio set to go on the other end, and built a one-valver. Bits and bobs were not easy to come by, but in the window of a shop in Mill Lane I spotted a second-hand variable condenser – the bit you twiddle to tune in – and a friend gave me a transformer, and I was in business with Marconi. Eventually, a bit of the Home (or was it the Forces?) Programme did emerge, and I was well pleased.

One thing leads to another, and with a copy of Wireless World I acquired a sixpenny booklet called Learning Morse. This included information on a one-valve practice set without which, it was represented, no one could learn the code. It became therefore the ambition of my life to have one. The booklet gave full details of how to build it, together with a list of parts required. It was rather ambitious, so Mr Bill Warren, a friendly chap whose wife kept Broken Cross Post Office and who dabbled in radio, offered to build it for me if I could get the bits.

Armed with my list I set off to tour the radio shops of Macclesfield but got stuck at the very first item. The book said: 'One AF choke 3H tapped'. This might as well have been written in Chinese, and meant nothing to me. Nor, I suspect, to most of the experts I consulted. I tried Mr Corbishley, who had a wireless shop in Westminster Street next to the public conveniences, which was handy because he practised also as a plumber. He too was concerned to help me, but after much scratching of the head, couldn't. I wound up my pilgrimage at McClure and Whitfield, a fairly large radio shop at 18 Mill Street, opposite Castle Street. Here I was served by a lady. I said I wanted an AF choke 3H tapped. She paused, and then said in a kindly way: 'I should try a garage – they'll fix you up with that sort of thing'.

I thereupon lost all confidence in radio shops, and gave up hope for my practice set. Dot dot dot dash dash dash dot dot dot.

Anyway, back to Aladdin's caves. The most cave-like of all were the establishments operated by salvage experts or metal reclaimers or – to speak plainly – rag and bone men. I became familiar with several of these, the best that I remember being a smelly haunt in Waterside, and a scrapyard in Swettenham Street at the top of Brook Street. Why did I visit these places, you will ask. The answer is simple. I needed pram wheels, naturally. EVERY boy needs two pairs of pram wheels, else how can he hope to build the trolley with which he can swoop down hillsides and neighbourhood pavements?

Well then, these items had to be sought out. In wartime there were scarcely any new prams, so second-hand wheels were like gold. I eventually acquired one pair in Waterside, and one pair (along with a car steering wheel) in Swettenham Street. The trolley was built and pronounced satisfactory, but it came to a sad end. One day I dismantled it for overhaul, and while it was in this vulnerable state my grandmother decided to have a clear-up and put the wheels out with the rubbish. No doubt they found their way back to another rag and bone man and were (ahem) recycled.

So much then for what you might call the lower end of my shopping excursus. It is now with great pleasure that I turn to the more upmarket world of toy shops.

In my opinion as an expert, the best of all the Macclesfield toy shops was Tom Wood's, halfway down Mill Street and next to Morley's. What Wild's in Lewis's Arcade was to Manchester, Tom Wood's was to Macclesfield. Of course, some might say that it was only half a toy shop, since the other half (the counter on the left as you pushed open the door) was a chemist's. Strange combination indeed. However, what could be found on the other side made up for all. I recall shelves crammed with all that heart of boy could desire. Toys on show and in plentiful supply ranged from the pocket money trifles – small Dinky ships could be bought for one old penny each – to the spectaculars coveted for birthdays and Christmas.

Such treasures included Meccano kits to build cars and planes – these change hands now for hundreds of pounds – and boxed sets of Dinky cars and lorries and Hornby trains. Dinky cars to be sold individually came to the retailer in cardboard boxes containing half a dozen of each type. It was a moment of breath-taking anxiety while Mr Wood examined his stock to see if he had just what you wanted.

Further up the street, especially at Christmas, was another delightful shop. Halfords, then at the corner of Exchange Street, laid in extra supplies of toys for this spending spree. One Christmas Eve my grandparents drove us into town and parked outside Halfords in Mill Street, facing up the hill as one could then. Inside the shop my brother was offered a bicycle, and chose one. Being younger I was content with a Hornby train set in its big blue box. By the time these purchases were completed night had fallen but the question remained: How were these gifts to reach Henbury in time for the morrow? The question was easily solved and the shop boy, poor lad, was called forward. When the store closed late at night he tied the train box round him, mounted the new bike and pedalled it to Henbury. He then had to be given a shilling so he could catch the bus home. I often wondered: What did he have for Christmas?

MCF.42F.   Market Place. Macclesfield.

Market Place in its days as the hub of a busy shopping centre with Boots on the right, Marks and Woolworths just down Mill Street, and the crowded market stalls themselves.

There was also a goodly supply of toys, ranged in regular and inspiring ranks, in Woolworths, that impressive store with its solid mahogany counters and large mirrors on the wall and, when I first knew it, gaslights. Here one could spend many happy hours browsing and, as nothing cost more than sixpence, there was always something to be bought if it was only a penny lead soldier.

There was one snag, however. The Woolworth technique at that time was to have island counters, with sometimes just one girl and one till trapped inside, and up to two dozen eager hands in a ring outside holding out goods (with loose screws and nails to be counted out by the dozen) and beseeching the assistant to take their money. Eyes at the back of their heads, these girls seemed to have, as they tried their best to keep everyone happy.

Woolworth's lead toys taught me another of life's valuable lessons. One day my brother and I were each given two shillings – 24 pennies, as you will recall. We dropped into Woolworths and, in those military days, admired a large squad of lead sailors. As always, they were a penny each. Philip adventured all his two shillings and acquired 24 of them. I wanted to cling on to my silver coin for a little longer, and said I would return after dinner. When I did – I tell no lie – it was to find that every blessed lead toy in the place had gone up to three ha'pence. Very sadly I handed over my florin and received – as you will work out – only 16 sailors to my brother's 24. The lesson, which I have tried to apply ever since, is to buy things when first you see them.

Talking of the number of lead soldiers and sailors reminds me that war was coming, and as it did the supply of metal toys dwindled. Finally at the end of 1941 their sale was banned altogether so that more important things like Spitfires and battleships could be built. What were Tom Wood and his colleagues to do? How sad his shelves looked now, with very few toys. One thing he could sell were the model aircraft kits I mention in the chapter on war. One Christmas, having been very generously treated, I decided to splurge seven shillings and sixpence (37½p) on what the box claimed was a flying model of a Spitfire. This was a very adventurous move. As I walked out of the shop, starry-eyed, I met a school friend and could not resist showing him my treasure. Together, on the pavement of Mill Street, we examined the contents – horrifyingly complex plans detailing spars and flanges, formers and spacers, wheels and propeller, all to be cut out of sheets of balsa wood. We gazed at it in silence for a while. 'You'll never make that', he said at last. And do you know, I never could.

With toys in such short supply one had to take one's pleasures where one could – we were reduced to hoarding such items as handfuls of 'chaff', the strips of metallised card which bombers dropped over Germany to confuse their radar. This was made in some of Macclesfield's war factories, and could be begged from friendly staff.

One also had to keep one's eyes open, for things cropped up in the most unlikely places – shops after all had to sell anything they could get. One day I walked down Chestergate and there in the window of an outfitter' shop – I think it was Ward's – and alongside a couple of ties and perhaps a pair of braces, I spotted three rather crude lead models of the American Flying Fortress bomber. Somehow they must have evaded the defenders of the Government's metal toy regulations. I rushed in and bought one. Sadly, it was shot down long ago, but recently I saw its cousin at a flea market and bought it, for old time's sake.

Next in order of popularity were sweetshops. Looking back it is astonishing how small some of them were – little more than the front room of a cottage with the sash window used to display goods. There was one on the corner of Langford Street and Chester Road, I remember, whose window display seemed to consist of four saucers of assorted sweets. Shops like that – there was another in Crompton Road, and one in Nelson Street – seemed able to survive on the sale of ha'porths of wine gums or dolly mixtures. But not for long. Once again, war removed their staple trade, and the great sweet-eaters of the world were left looking for something to take their place.

We looked long and hard, and sometimes desperately. In our need for something to chew, anything edible and not actually disgusting was eagerly sought and gratefully eaten. There were sulphur tablets from Hadfields on the corner of Stanley Street, iodised throat pastilles from Bryans the chemist, next to Woolworths, and licorice root from Granellis. All these helped to fill an aching void. Poor Mr Granelli, who had no ice cream to offer, was also reduced to selling off his stock of wafers, offering a few at a time in his window in Chestergate. They were rapidly sold out.

Word of anything eatable reaching the shops was rapidly passed around. I once played hookey from school after a rumour among the boys that lemons had been spotted at a little grocer's in King Edward Street. By the time I got there, they had all gone.

Of course, everyone's favourite shops depend on their taste, and like everyone else's, mine changed with the years. When I started serious reading I became a regular customer at W H Smith's historic-looking shop in the Market Place. When lamentably I took up smoking, I enjoyed calling in at Chester Twemlow's little store next door. But it was a long time before I had any call on my own account to visit one of the town's many jewellers. However, I did have one notable excursion into the emporium on Sunderland Street, opposite the Jolly Sailor, of Alderman Albert Breese, one of the town's worthies and a noted jeweller.

As a reward for passing my school certificate my generous grandmother took me there to buy a wristwatch. I liked the idea, but as this was just after the war such trinkets were rather scarce. When our errand was explained the

One from the past: Susie Slack and daughter outside the tollbar shop and post office at the corner of London Road just before the Moss Estate took shape around it.

alderman, with an air of conferring a great favour, produced just one watch from his safe, held it out for our inspection, and awaited our enthusiastic acceptance. Unfortunately, even at that distance I could see the face of the watch was a vivid pink, and I jibbed at wearing such a cissy-looking creation. When my grandmother explained my reservations Alderman Breese had a classic businessman's response. 'Never mind the looks, Mrs 'Anson', he said. 'You just can't get 'em!'

Further gentle pressure, however, persuaded him to look again in his safe where he found a much more masculine, silvery creation. With that, as with most of my dealings in the shops of Macclesfield, I was well content.

3

Old School Ties

With the same logic that says my dad is better than your dad, most people regard their school as better than any other. Never mind the warts – it's loyalty that counts. Thus, those who went to St Paul's School or St George's, Duke Street or Mill Street, would say that theirs was the best school in Macclesfield. I sympathise with their views but they are wrong. Christ Church was the best, and I know because I went there.

That distinctive building with its square tower and a pyramid hat on top has now vanished from the middle of Great King Street, and on its site stands a block of flats. But curiously, across the road in Pinfold Street there still survives the little yard, one of three playgrounds of which the school could boast, where I first played cricket with a composition ball and a heaving bat. This I suppose is like losing Buckingham Palace but keeping the sentry box; still, we must be grateful for whatever remains to kindle memories.

I started there when I was five and the headmaster was Billy Lee – a man blessed with several daughters but with a stern reputation for discipline. Happily, we tenderer shoots were spared the direct evidence of his wrath for while he presided in the senior school upstairs, and sometimes whacks and squeals resounded there, we began downstairs out of direct earshot. The first class was taught by Miss Williamson, whom I still meet today at church functions as she is a stalwart of St Michael's. However, I cannot claim to have been taught by her because for some reason I started in the second class with Miss Davenport.

I hope she wouldn't take it amiss if I confess that I can't remember anything she taught me in that year. All I do recall is my first sense of betrayal at the ways of the world for one day the whole class were handed copies of a coloured book on Snow White which had been printed and dished out by a corned beef firm. But do you know, it was a great disappointment because it wasn't THE Snow White, the genuine Disney production with which I had fallen in love on a trip to London that year. This was an ersatz version with unrecognisable dwarfs, and I felt I had been cheated.

The next year, in Miss Whittaker's class, was more memorable as we began to spread our wings in several ways. Modest rebellion began to stir the air. We were forbidden, on pain of some terrible punishment, to climb the great fire escape which led from the playground at the front to the top floor. But when for a present I was given a 'Frog' flying model aeroplane, all glittering silver

Christ Church school, on the left, in Great King Street

and whirring propeller, it was natural that I wanted a good launching site so up the stairs we trooped. The flight was a success.

Rebellion of a more malign kind surfaced also in the classroom, where I was one of the monitors (ink monitors, form monitors, paper monitors, we all had a turn). At this time the standard punishment for minor offences was to be called to stand at the front of the class. When one day the teacher had to leave us for five minutes I was placed in charge. How terrible to think that the love of power can flourish even in a seven-year-old – and one destined for the church at that! But no sooner had Miss Whittaker left than I determined to exercise this power. One lad to whom I took a dislike – Malcolm Harwood was his name – was ordered by me to stand at the front. He grumbled but, to my surprise, obeyed. When the teacher returned she wanted to know what he had done. He said, Nothing. I was asked to explain, and blustered and fumbled. At length, I had to agree that he was entirely innocent, and I was banished from the class.

But don't things turn out in odd ways? I was spared further shame by the onset of a violent nose bleed. Miss Whittaker, and other teachers who had been apprised of my crime, now turned from their condemnation to soothe and comfort me. But it taught me a lesson, that power can be a source of mischief and has to be watched.

Christ ☧ Church

........./*Paul Mayfield*..........

WAS AWARDED A

First Prize

in........*Writing*..........

AT THE

Annual Exhibition of Handicraft

In Christ Church School, Macclesfield,

SATURDAY,........*Oct. 30*........19.*3.7*.

....*President.*

....*Secretary.*

Good grief! A prize for writing! But it was 1937.

So our learning advanced, in all sorts of ways, though not always reliably as things turned out. One of the books from which I must have read is before me now. It is called the Wide World Geography Reader, British Empire section, and is stamped 'Christ Church School'. Right at the front is a page in colour showing the Union Jack, and the other national flags of the home countries. There are two chapters near the front called: 'The causes of Britain's Greatness'. There are maps with great splodges of red, and pictures of lots of happy peoples from different lands. There is a table showing the countries added to the Empire in different years and how – mostly 'by conquest' or 'by occupation'. How natural and grand it all sounded then; how far away now.

A rather odd incident comes to mind also from this year. It was a firm belief among us, though never to be confirmed by events, that if a whole class could get through all ten morning and afternoon sessions in one week without any absences, we would be rewarded at the end of the year by an extra half-holiday. This sounds easy to do, but proved remarkably elusive, hard though we tried. The week beginning Monday August 8, 1938, seemed to be our lucky one. We reached the Friday morning still without any absences, and only the afternoon to go. We could do it! But we couldn't. A violent thunderstorm hit the town that morning – a minor annoyance for us, a catastrophe for others, for in the thunder that rolled round our heads on August 12 a lightning bolt hit Peter Davenport's mill on Bridge Street, a quarter of a mile away, setting it on fire.

Class of 38 at Christ Church. Second from the right in the front row is the future curate, with friends
Alan Potts and Don Pearson on either side.

One employee, Doris Rogers, was unable to flee the blaze, and died. There
was extensive damage to the mill.

Back at Christ Church we were a sober band of survivors in the afternoon.
Many were missing – some kept at home by anxious parents as the rain poured
down, some sneaking a look at the firemen still working on the smoking
timbers, some too shocked by this intrusion of violence and grief into our cosy
world. We never did qualify for that extra holiday.

One last year downstairs – this time with Miss E Brough, the headmistress,
who lived in Chester Road. We put a final polish to our writing and multiplication tables, made paper chains and Chinese lanterns at Christmas, listened
occasionally to the new marvel of wireless for schools. Then it was upstairs
to Mr Lee's domain. I was only here for a month or so before moving on to
King's, but I do remember one awesome morning when Mr Lee was called
upon to exercise both his discipline and his cane, and this time we were close
at hand. Work in the class came to a halt as the sound of a verbal storm and
furious blows of the cane fell around us, followed by screams. We never found
out what the lad had done, but I don't suppose he was in any hurry to do it
again. I think of this incident because later on I acquired the clock from the
headmaster's room, the clock that ticked away the seconds of agony for the
unfortunate boy.

Soon after that I bade farewell to Christ Church. Our closest rivals had been

Athey Street school a couple of streets away, and whenever we passed its railings we would jeer at its lads from a safe distance. But you see who had the last laugh. Christ Church school is gone, but Athey Street lives on under its new name of Parkroyal. So much for jeering.

I was proud to move to King's, but also a bit in awe for it was a much vaster enterprise – 600 boys but no girls (I was too young to miss them); four separate major buildings; and a regiment of distinguished and at first rather remote teachers. Oh yes, and THE PREFECTS who were very lordly figures to a young boy.

It was all too much for me to go through my career there year by year, beyond saying that once again I started one rung off the bottom, missing form 1A which was presided over by Mrs Joyce Haworth. I renewed acquaintance with her in later life. As a matter of fact I conducted her funeral service, but as I said then I still could not think of her other than as Mrs Haworth, and I was quite sure she regarded me as Maybury of 2B.

In that form, under Mrs Titterton, of Broken Cross, we began our curriculum. We read Wind in the Willows, and worked our way up the school to Macbeth. In maths what started with multiplication ended with trigonometry and mechanics. Nature study blossomed into chemistry and physics. All this took seven years and the combined efforts of the headmaster, the renowned T T Shaw, and his team. They were mostly men, but in the war, with many called up for the services, the ranks had to be stiffened by a few women, and not only in the junior school. We had lessons (eagerly looked forward to) from Sheila Cregeen, the attractive daughter of a local Methodist minister. A Miss Hoather joined us to take the place, temporarily, of Selwyn Russell-Jones our talented and much respected art master. The redoubtable figure of Miss Marshall, reputed to be the sister of a doctor, even presided for some time over our PT sessions in the gym, to the grumbles of boys who declined to take a shower while there was any chance of her watching.

The masters too had some interesting characters among them, none more put upon than our senior mathematics teacher. In the prospectus he appeared as G C Bartindale MA, Scholar of Balliol College, Oxford, with first class honours in mathematical moderations and first class honours in mathematical finals. But to one and all of the boys he was simply Jim Crow. This lamentable nickname arose from the tattered appearance of his gown, but that was not his fault. The truth of the matter is that it was tattered because class after class of boys had, over the years, surreptitiously snipped pieces off it as he strode up and down the aisles in the classrooms. Whether his head was so stuffed full of equations that he never noticed, or whether he was simply too polite to stop the practice, none knew.

Our efforts were not of course restricted to scholastic endeavours. Much

The King's School, just after the war.

energy was expended on snowballing and sliding in the winter, impromptu athletics in the summer. More disciplined were the activities of assorted clubs and societies. With a racing cycle, purchased amid great excitement from Mr Brough in the Waters, I was a co-founder of the King's School Wheelers and went youth hostelling for holidays. I dabbled in photography with the photographic club, and chess with the chess club. Most tastes were catered for, and if enthusiasms soon waned at least we had some interesting experiences.

With the King's School Players I made two appearances in my final years, acting in Shaw's The Devil's Disciple and, more popularly, Agatha Christie's Ten Little Niggers (now called And Then there were None, but that's another story). The plays were directed by Mr M L 'Len' Harvey, who taught French and later became deputy head. Parts in the plays were much prized since, at the twice-weekly rehearsals and on performance nights, we were given an excellent tea by the catering staff. What boys will do for grub!

All sorts of weird things are likely to happen in a school. One day Mick Wright, son of the local vet, turned up with a dead monkey. It turned out that it had (in its living state, of course) bitten another friend, David Maurice, and paid the penalty. I believe it ended up in the biology lab, but we were too squeamish to inquire further.

I suppose that the annual hockey match between the burly heroes of King's rugby team, and the more demure girls of the High School, could also be described as interesting. . For this fixture large quantities of boys poured up

The King's School Players in Ten Little Niggers, 1947. Standing on the left is Mr M L Harvey, the play's producer and later deputy head of the school, who took over the leading part of the judge at short notice when F P Unwin was taken ill.

Buxton Road and along Fence Avenue anxious to spur on their team. We had a war cry which went like this, fortissimo:

BOOMeracka BOOMeracka BOOMeracka we,
Who are Who are Who are we?
We are
K I N G apostrophe S
KINGS!

I wish I could give you some of the results of these encounters, but I don't suppose they were of any importance compared with the chance we had of mixing ever so decorously with the girls we knew, looking around their school, and perhaps catching a glimpse of the redoubtable headmistress, Miss H G Walker.

There were more formal games of course – rugby was played by all though not well by many, if you see what I mean. I was one of the many, preferring soccer which was frowned on by the public school element among the King's

MASTERS.

Head Master: F. D. EVANS, M.A., Scholar of Brasenose College, Oxford. First Class Classical Moderations. Second Class Lit. Hum., Late Assistant Master at Merchiston Castle, Edinburgh.

Senior Assistant Master: E. T. S. TADMAN, B.A., London, First Class.

E. WITHERS, B.A., Corpus College, Cambridge.

M. W. DAVIES, B.A., Scholar of Christ Church, Oxford. Lit. Hum. Second Class Honours. Final School of Modern History, Second Class Hons.

T. H. LEADBETTER, B.A., Liverpool, F.R. Met. S.

F. C. MILNER, B.A., London.

T. OWEN, B.Sc., Liverpool.

R. B. RAWSTHORN, M.Sc., Manchester University. Second Class Honours in Chemistry.

C. E. KEMP, B.Sc., London.

C. H. HAYLETT, M.A , Birmingham.

The Rev. R. B. I. SHARPE, M.A., London. Second Class Honours in Classics.

G. C. BARTINDALE, M.A., Scholar of Balliol College, Oxford. First Class Honours, Mathematical Moderations. First Class Honours, Mathematical Finals.

J. W. E. RANSLEY, B.Sc., London.

M. CAIGER, M.A., Manchester University. Second Class Honours in French.

M. STORRS FOX, Emmanuel College, Cambridge. Second Class Honours in History.

S. TAYLOR, B.A., Queen's College, Cambridge. Second Class Honours in Physics. B.Sc. London, Second Class Honours.

Drawing & Manual Instruction: S. J. POINTING.

Music: E. G. GULLIFORD, A.R.C.O.

Gymnastics: Sergt. Major J. DEVREY, K.O.S.B.

3

King's School masters listed in a prospectus in the 1930s

masters. I did leave a tiny mark, mostly circular, in the cricket scorebooks, playing four matches for the very junior under-fourteens team. The coaching and help I received from the cricketing giants of the school – Freddie Millett, Gil Manssuer and John Higginson, who will be mentioned later on in this book – failed to improve my game and my experience was such as to dash any hope I had nurtured that I might one day play for England.

But of all the events the most riotous and the most anticipated was the annual Christmas soiree for the sixth form. As you worked your way up the school tales of this extravaganza, heavily embroidered, filtered down from the seniors lucky enough to attend. And then at last it was our turn – and it all proved to be true. Japes were played – underpants and chamberpots appeared mysteriously on the school flagpole. One year a dainty little car belonging to one of the masters – Mr Curphy of chemistry, I think – was picked up and planted crossways in a narrow passage with a brick wall at each side, so it could not be removed without being picked up again and by then all the boys had gone.

In the hall there was entertainment of a mildly risque and embarrassing kind, and some of the staff went through their party pieces. Supper was served by the masters, led by T T Shaw. There were many ribald comments on their appearance and their waiting abilities, and knowing it happened but once a year they appeared to take it in good part.

There was, however, a limit to the insults they were prepared to take on other occasions. During the annual School v Staff cricket match I was with a

Nearest rival to King's geographically – Beech Hall School in the 1930s

party of fifth formers who wished to enliven the proceedings with comments on the masters' performance. From the safety of the boundary we kept up a barrage of catcalls, and felt ourselves so witty. Halfway through the school innings, the masters went into a huddle. 'Perhaps they're changing the field', we said. 'Perhaps they'll move mid-off a bit deeper'. But what they were planning to move was us. Their spokesman was 'Ben' Davies, English master and chief cricket coach, who now strode over and ordered us back into school and we left with bowed heads to the accompaniment of boos and jeers, reporting to him later for a telling off. Next time we had something to say we were careful to moderate our voices.

From our redoubt in Cumberland Street we didn't have a great deal of contact with other schools in the town. The next largest in size was I suppose the Central School (now St Barnabas) which was presided over by the formidable Mr R E Houseman. My grandparents were socially on speaking terms with him but, owing to his reputation for discipline, I did not wish to be.

Our nearest neighbours geographically were the boys of Beech Hall school on the slopes of Tytherington, just across the Bollin from the bottom of our playing fields. We came closest to them on our annual purgatorial cross-country race. The course dropped down to the Bollin, then along the river valley past Beech Hall until, level with Bollinbrook, it crossed the river again (with much splashing), and climbed the hill back to the end of Westminster Road where the first prefabs were just being erected. From there it was a slog back along the pavement to the playing fields and safety. Perhaps it was two miles altogether. It felt much longer.

Talking of Beech Hall reminds me of our respective colour schemes, for the boys there wore bright red caps and blazers. King's wore bright blue, and the Central School green. What a colourful lot we would have been had we ever got together, but as far as I know we never did.

4

Tiddlers, Toads And Bluebells

In Church Lane at Henbury, on the right just past the semi-detached houses, you can still see an old farm gate leading into a field. And whenever I pass it I remember that this used to be the entrance to a land of great enchantment.

For next to the gate there was a style, and beyond that, on the edge of a cornfield where the houses of Henbury Rise now stand, there was a path, and fifty yards down that path there was a pond which in many senses was our happy hunting ground. The attraction needs really no explanation. As cream cakes are to some ladies, so is stagnant water to the inquiring boy. What pleasures do its depths contain, what mysteries? Well, I can tell you some of the mysteries of the Henbury pond, for we delved into them.

Arriving there often in the early morning, when there was a hushed and eerie haze waiting for the sun to burn it away, we would first lie down by the water's edge and stir up its soupy contents. At the right times of the year this would reveal large patches of the spawn of frog and toad, and this lamentably we would scoop into the jamjars we had (always optimistically) brought with us. These we carried home, and in due course we had before our eyes a biology lesson, for the spawn turned of course into tadpoles and then tiny froglets. Alas, that ended both our interest and the froglets, for we tipped them out and few could have survived.

But back at the pond there was further exploration waiting. We saw, without bothering to learn their names, dragonfly and butterfly, and the curious insects that seemed able to skate on the surface of the water. All was magical. As the sun rose, and with it our temperatures, we removed shoes and socks and took tentative steps in the ooze, feeling around with our feet in case there might be buried treasure or at least an old bike, but we got nothing save a few cuts.

Thereafter, as the morning wore on, we sought other amusement, and there was at least one close to hand. Further along the path stood a pair of cottages, improbably sited in glorious isolation midway between Church Lane and Whirley Road, and having at that time no access for a car. Their inhabitants had a walk of a quarter of a mile in any direction to reach a road. One of these cottages was of particular interest to those of us connected with the church, for it had been made available as a home for the Revd David Thomas, our priest in charge during the war. As is the way of young people with their heroes, we would after our dredgings in the pond find ourselves attracted to the cottage, and hang around outside it in the hope that he would emerge and occupy another few minutes for us.

Henbury Hall in its earlier and homelier incarnation

Visits to this pond were not our only encounters with acquatic life. Down Andertons Lane there was another pond to which we often repaired. This was definitely a better class of pond for it lay in a hollow between two imposing houses – The Mount and Whirley Rise. The former was for three years at the turn of the century the home of the Revd John Wade. He is of some fame because he was the immediate successor at Haworth of the Revd Patrick Bronte and stayed in that parish for 37 years before retiring to Henbury. At the Rise lived Freddie Bradley, School Captain at King's during my time there and a hero of the school's first cricket eleven.

In this little pool we took our first and totally unsuccessful steps in angling, usually ending up with our titchy little lines in a tangle. But it did have other uses. Bobby Hunter's father Stanley – later to take over the Carswell lorry firm in the town – had built for him a substantial ship out of biscuit tins. Perhaps the years have increased its bulk, but we regarded it then with some awe as being not far short in size of a hull a-building on Cammell Laird's slipway. Clutching this monster we staggered one day to the pond to see if it would float. After a ceremonial launch, it did. Thereafter we lost interest in it.

The last of the ponds to engage our attention was a small one down Whirley Lane, between Whirley Hall and the main Chelford Road. By this time I had blamed my lack of angling success on my equipment, and so for a sum not exceeding half a crown I had purchased from a shop in Commercial Road a little, basic cane rod. This I took to the Whirley pool and – success! Out of its shallows I hooked a poor little silver dace (that's what my knowledgeable

Luxuriant growth at Bluebell Wood, Henbury

colleagues said it was) and took it home in the inevitable jamjar as a trophy. For two days it swam around, and then perished. That almost quenched my enthusiasm.

But not quite. I had one more card to play in my engagement with the fish. We knew there was a lake in the grounds of Birtles old hall, a genuine lake and not a tiddly pond. There we went with our rods, and sat very damply in a persistent rain. I had just landed a perch about this big when a member of the hall's household arrived and, do you know, he charged us each sixpence for using the lake! That was another lesson in life, not to take these things for granted. Oh, and the fish lay in state on a plate at home for a whole day before its deterioration became unmistakable, and it was buried in the garden.

Not all our adventures with nature involved the animal world; we also had our fitful enthusiasms for plant life, or simply for lolling around in the country sunshine. We made a desultory study of the wildflowers, growing so plenti-fully then in the farmers' hedgerows where we felt free to wander at will. I once won a school prize for my collection of pressed flowers, but now I couldn't tell a vetch from a celandine. One flower we didn't need to learn anything about, however, was the bluebell, since we had our own local bluebell wood. This was down the lane from the Blacksmith's Arms, on the way to Redesmere, and almost opposite Henbury Hall. At this time the hall was a rather homely 19th century creation, the residence of the Brocklehurst family, though it has now been replaced by a Palladian mansion with dome and is the home of Sebastian de Ferranti. In this little wood, quite remote and unmolested by any censorious passers-by in that tolerant age, we gathered our bluebells by the armful and felt no pang of conscience.

We had also a larger wood for our playground, shown on the Ordnance map as Cock Wood though to us it was simply The Wood. We reached this by dropping down the hill at the back of Putty Row – begging its pardon, Pleasant View, a row of cottages on Chelford Road. Then by crossing a little bridge we reached our adventure ground where trees were to be climbed and the stream dammed and tunnels to be dug. The stream, which we could wade along for half a mile, formed the boundary between Henbury and Macclesfield, crossed beneath Chelford Road and then wended its way over the fields towards Whirley and out of our own domain.

These then were the glorious days in our part of the country – the long, hot and roving days. Sometimes when we were lucky on our ramblings we encountered the Walls ice-cream man, laboriously pedalling his blue tricycle along the dusty road and inviting us to stop him and buy one. What we usually bought was half a triangular Snofruit – precursor of the ice-lolly – for one ha'penny. To win such custom he had sweated for at least two miles getting out of town, and would have to pedal two miles back. He must have wondered if the gods of employment had been kind to him.

These scenes from Macclesfield include two from the village of Prestbury, now noted for the number of resident millionaires but then regarded simply as a playground for the boys and for afternoon teas at the Bollin Cafe. Bottom left, the Walls ice cream man wearily pedals his welcome wares.

But there were other days too to be relished in the country – just as exciting but a lot colder and shorter. These were winter days, when the ponds froze and we could slide on them, and the fields turned white and we could sledge on them. Although we lived on the level side of the town we were lucky enough to have the use of at least three good, fast sledging tracks – Brick Bank and Gorse Track in Cock Wood, and the Sandpit on Chelford Road. The first were quite isolated and quiet and saw mostly small parties of two or three dedicated sledgers; Sandpit was more public, being in full view of the road and, more interestingly, with ten houses at the bottom whose gardens you might demolish if you failed to hang out your right leg and turn the sledge in good time. In one of these houses lived Winifred Bracegirdle, noted elsewhere in these pages as a pianist and singer, but one day she must have been overwhelmed by the noise and high spirits coming from the hill behind her for she came out and spent the morning begging lifts on the speeding sledges.

Yes, great fun it all was. But even before childhood was over we had realised that the country was not a playground for everyone, and we saw at close hand the toil of farmers for whom the land was their livelihood. Our observations started gently enough with the farm across the road. This was kept by Mr Buxton and his daughter Nellie one of whom had each day, sometimes before we were up and about, to push their milk-churn-on-wheels from house to house, ladling out milk into the quart cans which people left at their gates. Before long, welcome or not, we began to visit the shippon and see the milking going on, twice a day, seven days a week, without a holiday for cow or farmer.

So we learned early that the farmers who came to church to thank God for their harvest had also their own hard part to play in creation and growth. And also, there could at times be tragedy. One day in our garden we looked across Mr Buxton's field and saw him standing with Nellie and a strange man and, even at that distance, they looked dejected. Then we saw a cow, dying or already dead, we could not quite make out, but there was a great loss for a small farmer to bear.

However, he played his part in my education. We puzzled for a long time, for example, over the mystery of the large pump on which he depended for his water supply. This gushed forth, when treated right, into a large stone trough but – what made it gush? How strange it was that it had to be primed, that water had to be emptied into the top of the pump before working the handle produced more water out of the bottom. It simply wasn't logical – but it worked.

One principle which didn't, and I can vouch for this, was the principle of centrifugal force. We had read in one of our boy's rather woolly magazines – the kind that also said you could cut glass under water with a pair of scissors but we never could – that you could swing a bucket of water round your head without spilling a drop. All you had to have was confidence and sufficient velocity. A bucket seemed a bit beyond us, but when Philip and I were sent across to the farm for an extra pint of milk in a can, we seemed to have the answer to hand. We swung with all our might.

I truly believe that whoever claimed to have invented centrifugal force was deliberately misleading young boys.

There was more hard work, but spiced with great interest, when harvest time brought out the threshers. This interesting season was heralded, usually while we were still at breakfast, by a deep chugging rumble approaching on the road outside, which could only be the threshing machine convoy. This outfit was provided – for the pleasure of young boys, we firmly believed – by the Barlows who lived by the sandpit. Pulling it along was a steam traction engine, followed by a threshing machine, a towering wooden castle on wheels, and behind this trailed a baler. The whole thing was noisy, slow and enormous. If we were quick we could rush out, grab our bikes and catch up this caravan before it plunged into one or other of the lanes leading to a farm. How the driver negotiated some of the twisting tracks between high hedges is a mystery, but get there he did, and soon there would be a line of boys watching entranced from the nearest hedgerow as the engine's pulley turned a belt which operated the thresher which rattled and shook until from somewhere out popped a bale of hay, while a stream of corn was directed into sacks.

The machine was fed with sheaves of corn from on top, and they had therefore to be pitchforked up from ground level. One or two kindly farmers let us try our hands at this hard labour. One of these was Ike Powell, who lived at Henbury but who farmed at Nether Alderley, and when the grapevine told us it was his turn to get in the corn, thither we scooted. It was on one of his farms that a class of us were given lessons in milking – without much success – and it was in the orchard behind his house at Henbury that I dined one sunny afternoon on unripe pears, and suffered a terrible penalty.

Eventually the two sides of country life – enjoyment and dashed hard work – came together in my case in the activity known as potato picking. During the war it seemed sensible to those in authority to ask young schoolboys and girls, bursting with energy, to help out the hard-pressed farmers with their potato crop for a week or a fortnight a year. How could we refuse time off, and be paid for it, too? Consequently, after a day's trial picking with some friends at Gawsworth I was passed as competent and was free to choose a farm on which I could spend a week. In the next three years I lent my talents to Prestbury Lane Ends farm, Newton Hall farm at Mottram, and Cocks Moss farm at Marton.

I can truthfully say it was the hardest graft I have known before or since. The farmers (it seemed to us) had the bobby's job, for they sat on the tractor towing a potato grubbing machine along the rows of plants. The boys, stationed at regular intervals along the row, had to pick up the potatoes in baskets and rush them to the earth clamps for storage. The farmers insisted on starting the next row before we had finished the last one, so there was a mad scramble. In potato terms, the farmer was King Edward and we were common Cheshires. It was a continuous flurry until the cavalry hove in sight – the farmer's wife arrived with the basket of 'bagging', or sandwiches and hot drinks, and we had quarter of an hour's respite before starting again.

Of course, I exaggerate. Hard work it may have been, but it was also good fun *and* we got paid 4s 6d a day or 25s if we stayed for a full five-day week (some lesser souls didn't). The farmers also paid in other ways. We had glorious games in the farmyards at lunch time, and I remember at Lane Ends we invented a competition for sliding down the hayrick, which resulted in a lot of hay being scattered about. The farmer, stumbling on this scene of devastation, declared that 'you young beggars are more trouble than you're worth'. I had to agree.

At least we avoided the shame of a party of pickers we knew from the High School for Girls. They landed up at a farm in Whirley where the farmer's wife, under the impression that she was entertaining a group of genteel and well-connected young ladies, put them in her parlour at lunchtime and served tea in her best china. One cup fell and was smashed – a tragedy in those wartime days when quality china could not be replaced. After that it was mugs, and the barn.

Even more ambitious than potato picking was the King's School decision one year to help out a group of farmers with their harvest. Volunteers for a harvest camp at Chester were called for, and though I was judged too young to do the farmwork (such nonsense) a family lobby persuaded the head to let me go and help in the camp kitchen. Thereafter plans on the scale of a Himalayan expedition were put in train. Tents were hired, with kitchen ranges and all the paraphernalia necessary to sustain 50 or 60 lads and their teachers for a fortnight without starving.

When the day arrived we cycled the 35 miles to Chester – an ordeal in itself – and then got to work. However, I survived only two days among the camp stoves and the strange odours before I took to my sleeping bag in the tent whose canvas I can still smell. A doctor had to be summoned, and it was decided that the long-suffering head, T T Shaw, should take me home in his Ford Pilot car, the bicycle to follow later. There was some concern that I had appendicitis, but I suspect it was a surfeit of what the German master, pressed into service as the camp cook, described grandly as camp mayonnaise. The boys had a different name for it.

5

Here We Go Into the White/Blue Yonder ...

On certain magical mornings in summer, when the sun was shining (as it always did, you remember), a little family group would stand outside the Cock Inn at Henbury and strain its eyes up the gently rising half-mile of road to Broken Cross.

What were we waiting for? What was it that my mother and grandmother, brother and I all longed to see? Ah, I can feel the excitement still – we were looking out for the first sign of the white and blue chara that was coming to pick us up and take us, with 20 or 30 other eager souls, on a day trip to Blackpool.

For some reason on these occasions we had a fierce loyalty to the firm of John Eccles and Son, whose family in the thirties kept the Derby Arms Hotel in Chestergate, opposite Wellings the chemist, and also had a coach depot in the yard there.

The town had other coach companies, of course, notably Dewhurst Brothers, who kept their coaches, hearses and funeral cars in a yard next to the Pack Horse hotel in Jordangate. And occasionally Wells of Biddulph and Bostocks of Congleton were called in by Macclesfield people.

But it was invariably the coaches of Mr Eccles that sprang to mind when we felt the call of the sea, and his coaches alone that we hopped aboard with such alacrity as they kept their morning rendezvous outside the Cock Inn. There were so far as we knew just two coaches in the fleet, and much of the success of the day – for the boys at any rate – depended which one came to pick us up. One coach was what you might call the standard sort, with the driver in a cab and the radiator more or less level with the front. The other, the one we hoped to see, was altogether smaller with the radiator sticking out at the front, and the driver not segregated but sitting there in full view for all the world as though he were driving our family car.

The attraction of this coach rather than the other will be obvious. And especially was our day made if we had been allocated the front seat on the left-hand side of this coach. For this gave us the great pleasure of watching every move the driver made – how he changed gear, when he pressed on the accelerator, how he operated the lights at night. This, you might say, was our first driving lesson. For example, watching his actions as he changed up

THE
NORTH WESTERN
Road Car Co., Ltd.

Luxurious Motor Char-a-Bancs

AND

Saloon Omnibuses

FOR

Private Hire for Outings,

Dances, Football Matches,

Theatre Parties, Etc.

Let Us Quote You.

Full particulars and prices
on application at the Office.

KING EDWARD STREET.　　G. CARDWELL,
MACCLESFIELD　　　　　　MANAGER.
PHONE 276.

An early advertisement when the North Western garage
was in King Edward Street – and the phone had only
three digits.

NORTH WESTERN
Road Car Co. Ltd.

SINGLE

STAGE BOARDED

Its fare paid.

| 1d |
| 2d |
| 3d |
| 4d |
| 5d |
| 6d |
| 7d |
| 8d |
| 9d |
| 10d |
| 11d |
| 1/- |
| 1/- |

7736

Oc86

The long tickets that caused some
wartime grumbles

through the gears, and then stopped at traffic lights, I fell to wondering why it took three shifts of the lever to get into top, but only one to get back again. So, I discovered the principle of neutral, accessible from all gears, and I felt I deserved the Nobel prize.

Let us then imagine that we are settled in this prized front seat, the driver releases the handbrake, and off we move up the little hill and on past Henbury church. Until we get to Chelford we keep looking around us, but soon we get bored because the driver isn't doing very much except steering, so our thoughts drift away a bit. Knutsford we notice briefly, and then Warrington, where there is the chance of excitement because, if we are lucky, we shall find we have to stop so the big swing bridge can open to let traffic through on the ship canal, and we can have a grandstand view of a ship like the side of a cliff swishing

Dewhurst ad from just after the war

past. I don't suppose the driver was so thrilled at having to wait, but soon we are off again and now we can look forward to the next adventure at Chorley.

For it is here that we pull up to enjoy the facilities of the Halfway House – not that there were too many in the war. I remember a great expanse of loose tarmac on which we gathered to stretch our legs, and a crush at the serving hatch for those who wanted a drink. What we got was tea – and wartime quality tea too – in a thick mug, with little milk and no sugar. Here let me say that I never, on perhaps a dozen such outings, saw any sign of the boozy chara trips so beloved of comic postcard artists and, nowadays, television comedy series. I will be prepared to swear that no crates of ale sullied the boot of our Eccles coach, and I never saw anyone take strong drink let alone be the worse for it. Perhaps I was too naive, or we were just moving in the wrong circles.

Impatient to be off, we soon climb back into the coach and move away on the last lap. Through the streets of Preston we go, and very soon after that begins the greatest game of all – who will be the first to spot Blackpool Tower? Philip and I vie for this honour, and the winner is rewarded with threepence.

So we arrive and are set down in the town, and get off to sniff the air like terriers let loose in the morning. It may seem strange if I digress to speak about Blackpool in a book about Macclesfield, but the fact is that for the annual Barnaby holiday the resort was like Macclesfield on Sea, with so many friends and neighbours from the town to be spotted and chatted to. At these times our local papers despatched reporters to the front, and without any trouble at all they could find an army of Silk Town folk enjoying themselves, and find out

John Eccles & Sons
RADIO COACHES

Motor Coach Tours

SUNDAY, June 29th—   Fare
2-30—**Monsal Dale & Chatsworth
Park** 5/-
2-30 & 7 p.m.—**Circular Tours 2/6**
WEDNESDAY, July 3rd—
7 p.m.—**Circular Tours** 2/6

All our Tours start from
DERBY ARMS GARAGE
CHESTERGATE, MACCLESFIELD.
Tel. 3075.

Eccles' delights – tours available in the thirties

what they were doing and send the news back to the office to appear in that week's paper. Sometimes in the great days, supplies of the *Times* or the *Courier* were actually sent to Blackpool, and sold on the prom.

Of course it wasn't always Barnaby on our day trips, but it was always Blackpool, and I had then – and still keep – a very special feeling for the place. First was its sense of freedom, from mundane things like school and, in an ever-so-gentle way, from family too. 'The boys' were spreading their wings and were increasingly trusted to enjoy themselves, and we did. We weren't great paddlers, nor even riders of the Grand National or the scenic railway. Our greatest joy was the Golden Mile, before it was tarted up a bit, and the piers. There one had all the fun of buying things we didn't really want from people who were just a little seedy, but finding it an adventure all the same. There was one character on the Central Pier who had a kiosk devoted to conjuring tricks and jokes in bad taste. He seemed to specialise in lapel badges which were really disguised water squirters, and these provoked much mirth if you could catch anyone out and spray them. One of these dribbling badges was a dog – 'A French dog', the huckster told his crowd, 'because if you press the bulb it goes oui oui!' This passed as a great and daring joke among the lads.

But Blackpool taught us other things apart from how to laugh. We stayed at this time in a hotel called the Victoria, on the North prom just before Uncle Tom's (it is now part of a larger hotel). Here, anxious not to waste a precious moment of holiday time at the start of our week, I got up one morning at 6.30, wandered downstairs, and there found a young girl, of perhaps 14 or 15, clearing out the grate in the lounge after last night's fire. It was a bit of a shock. Clearly I was on holiday, and she was not. That is how I learned that we all depend on one another, and those who care for us deserve in turn our consideration.

In the theatres which are so much a part of the Blackpool scene and where I saw, among others, George Formby and Gracie Fields, I learned that there is something magnetic and quite indefinable called star quality. Both these

NORTH PIER NEW PAVILION BLACKPOOL

Secretary   -   -   -   W. M. GIBSON.

LAWRENCE WRIGHT

Presents his 1941 Edition of

Devised by LAWRENCE WRIGHT.   Staged by WALTER M. MORRIS

Artistes include :

Soprano : **MARGARET EAVES.**

Baritone : **SIDNEY BURCHALL.**

Comedian : **DAVE MORRIS**, assisted by **BILL SMITH.**

Comedienne : **BERYL REID.**

Three Coloured Aristocrats : **THE NORMAN THOMAS TRIO.**

Design to Delight : **DON PHILLIPE and MARTA.**

New Star : **BEBE TERRY.**

Britain's Youngest Comedienne :
DOROTHY WILLIAMS.

Chorus : **TERRY'S PRIZE JUVENILES.**

By arrangement
with
Madame Terry

Gertrude Ainsworth's FESTIVAL DANCERS : **OLGA McMARTIN,
BETTY BOLD, PAULINE SIMONETT,
BETTY FERRIOR, KATHLEEN CARDWELL,
JOYCE LORD, PAT MARTIN.**

BRAM MARTIN and his Famous B.B.C. **BAND.**

DAILY AT 2-30 and 7-30.

SUNDAY CONCERTS at 7-30.

BOOK SEATS AT NORTH PIER, BLACKPOOL 980.

PROGRAMME   -   -   -   -   -   PRICE 2d.

Some of the joys awaiting the Blackpool visitor

entertainers, if you analysed their acts, were basically quite similar to hundreds of other performers down the bill. But the great have something extra that quite defies analysis, and the joy is in trying to recognise it in any walk of life.

And finally – well, finally I am indebted to Blackpool for a moment of revelation. Again with Philip, we rushed out of the hotel at about 8 o'clock in the morning, dashed across the prom, being careful to watch for trams, ran through the gardens, scrambled down the rock walks and so reached the beach. At that time of day we had it to ourselves. The cliff behind us hid the noise of the suburbs. To either side of us stretched what seemed illimitable sands; ahead

Workers from Hewetson's in Macclesfield on a day trip with Wells of Biddulph in the thirties.

of us, the even more unbounded ocean. For the first time I became aware of the vastness of creation. It came to me that there was a mighty creator. It dawned on me that there was God.

So this was the Blackpool, an old but lively friend, to which we said goodbye after our day trip, and with less excitement than in the morning we again boarded our white and blue coach. This time the run sped by mainly in a blur of weariness, for we were heavy with fresh air and rock and chips. And finally we were decanted at Henbury, a well pleased family.

Coaches were always regarded as the posh end of the bus trade, but in Macclesfield we were lucky to be served, day in and day out, on town roads and country lanes, by service buses that were not far short of chara standards. Our bus company was the North Western, born in Macclesfield but by this time based at Stockport and serving a web of routes in Cheshire, Derbyshire and Lancashire. It was a company renowned for its standards of comfort. Its seats were luxurious and well sprung, the lights had dainty glass shades, the windows had curtains. Most of its single-deckers – and Macclesfield was predominantly a single-deck fleet because of the low bridges which had to be negotiated – had an unusual 'porch' entrance at the back. This featured three fairly steep and enclosed steps with a door at the top which could be shut in cold weather.

Most of these buses also had what is known in the trade as half-canopy fronts. In these the roof line at the front covered the jutting-out cab, but then cut back to the line of the front passenger window behind the bonnet. This gave the bus a singularly lopsided and rather disconcerting look, as if the

Girl Guides led by Marion Braddock of St Barnabas (left) ready to set out on a Dewhurst coach for their annual camp in 1949

driver's side of the vehicle were nicely on time but the left-hand side was running late. But many North Western buses in other towns had for some reason the more logical full canopies in which the same roof line covered both the front of the cab and the space over the bonnet. You can see the difference in two pictures in this chapter: The Wells coach on the Hewetson outing is a full-canopy design: the North Western just creeping in at the end of the St George's Street Baptist procession is a half-canopy.

There was another reason why a ride in a North Western bus in Macclesfield had about it the air of a mini chara trip: most of the services had to start from the new bus station in Sunderland Street and take the scenic route through the Waters, along Gas Road by the gasworks, up Hibel Road past the station, and finally up Jordangate to the Market Place to the main town stop. This was the result of building, just before the war, a bus depot about 100 feet below the level of the busiest part of the town. There were no stops for the shopper in Mill Street, as there are now.

In the war, when buses were scarce and packed, passengers wanting to be sure of a seat were well-advised to trek down the hill to the bus station. Those who liked taking a risk, or who didn't have the energy for a long walk, queued in the Market Place but often found that the Manchester bus was already full when it got there, and that meant a half-hour wait for the next one.

The long start to the journey did have its advantages for the fleet-footed. Once four of us got on the bus at the station, and just as it was pulling out in Sunderland Street we saw brother Philip pelting along and trying to leap aboard. He failed, but was not defeated. He turned about, panted along the Waters and up Churchwallgate and *still* reached the Market Place stop just as the bus was pulling in. He climbed aboard to a rousing cheer.

Passengers in those days, and especially the young ones, had a fairly clear idea of how the bus service should be run – perhaps times have not altered much in this respect – and especially they disliked change. I remember boarding a bus at Henbury one day and being astonished to find seats down both sides facing inwards, with a large open space in between. This was a 'standee' bus, designed to cram in as many as possible standing up. It was quite chummy on a crowded bus, but you did have to like each other. I don't think the experiment lasted long.

Another innovation which caused grave mutterings was the introduction of what seemed to us huge tickets terribly wasteful at a time when everyone was being urged to save paper. These were the famous Willebrew tickets, a system which provided the conductor with a line of prices down the side of the ticket, which he could chop off in a special machine. The clippings were stored in the machine so that, back at the depot, the office staff could laboriously examine them and tot up exactly how much each conductor should be paying in. These cumbersome tickets remained in use for 12 or 15 years until machines which printed the appropriate fare on each ticket as it was issued were introduced.

As well as running luxurious buses, North Western expected a clean and tidy staff, and they wore neat dark blue uniforms with their badges – red border for the driver, green for conductors – looking like medals. Typical of the drivers was Bert Bolgere, who joined in 1946 and in his 21 years there won several safe-driving and long service awards. Like all the drivers he was called on for different types of duties, from the short Town Service and Lyme Green routes to the busy Manchester runs and the Derby expresses. I won't say the drivers were always heroes to us, but we did admire the way they could tug on the vast handbrake, and crash through the gears as they struggled up Hibel Road. All this we could watch eagerly through the glass at the back of their cab – they must have felt like goldfish.

Conductors too had their times of difficulty, especially on short, busy routes like the Moss Rose service which used double-deckers. There could be 60 or more passengers packed aboard, all of whom had to be approached, given change for their fare, and issued with a ticket. The conductor had about five

This picture of a St George's Street Baptist Church procession in the early 1950s is interesting for at least three of the reasons mentioned in this book: 1. It shows an attempt at smart dress on these occasions, though only a few are up to silk mill standards (see chapter 19).; 2. The big Backhouse and Coppock Mill in the centre may not have its chimney, but it still does have its tower, which has now been removed as part of the new lower-line Vertika mill (chapter 13); 3. The bus which is creeping in on the right is an archetypal half-canopy North Western single decker, running from either Lyme Green or Sutton (see this chapter).

minutes to do all this as the bus bounced and swayed, in addition to watching the passengers as they got on and off. On all journeys, standing with knees flexed to take the bumps, he had in between punching tickets to enter up his waybill giving details of fares received. And on top of all that, he was expected to answer queries about services by looking them up in his dinky company timetable with a little red bus on the front.

One of the conductors from this time, George Grice, told a story which illustrates the standard which passengers expected. George was trying to get his tickets issued on a crowded bus when he was berated by a woman passenger, who accused him of taking her past her stop. He pointed out that she hadn't rung the bell. She replied: 'But you KNOW I always get off there'.

Altogether, before the universal coming of the car, we seemed to spend so much of our time riding on buses, or noting their numbers like other boys went train spotting, or simply standing and admiring them. It was a lucky day when you found two of these orangey beasts trying to pass each other in crowded Chestergate – I could have watched for hours but all too soon one managed to inch through and the road was cleared again. Another vantage point was the bus stop in Chester Road, just past Archers the bakers. Here buses could come at you by two routes, depending on the service. One coming down Chestergate would simply poke its nose round the corner by the traffic lights, and there was nothing too exciting there. But the other would drive down King Edward Street, between the tunnel-like walls of the mills, and suddenly come popping out like a ferret from a drainpipe. It was a cheering moment, especially if you had been waiting a long time.

Such freedom, buses and charas seemed to give us – and for such a small price, too. Three ha'pence on the bus from Henbury to town, 2s 4d (12 new pence) return to Manchester. And on the charas there were mill outings, choir and Sunday School outings, and pub outings (now there at least you could expect the crates of beer). Hold very tight, please, to these memories.

6

The Sun's Hour of Rest

The 'insistent whisper' which led me into the church started off, I must say, at a very low volume, and it took a long time to become noticeable and an even longer one – 55 years! – to be irresistible.

But it was there, I recognise now, right from the start, as soon as I could hear anything at all, for the house where I was brought up echoed to the sound of hymns. My grandmother, as she dusted or cooked or washed up or simply tripped off to her dances or tennis, would warble hymns. They embraced the simple and durable – 'Shall we gather at the river?' – to the deep and now unheard – 'The voice of God's creation found me', and dozens of others in between. She was also, as most grandmothers are, full of wise and pithy sayings designed to keep the world on the right track. 'It's a sin to steal a pin', and 'Be sure your sin will find you out' were among the most regular that were called for in our upbringing.

It was therefore only to be expected that the boys made an early acquaintance with church. At first this was Christ Church, where my grandfather was

Henbury Church in the days when the caretaker's house, just visible between church and vicarage, still stood in Church Lane.

Stiff collars and dicky bows for the Henbury choirboys of 1940. Here are Philip Maybury (left) and Denis Earlam

a warden. The attraction here was to sit up in the balcony where our heads were at roughly the same level as the head of Mr Sharples when he eventually popped up at the top of the huge pulpit to preach. We were almost eyeball to eyeball. My word, that was a monster pulpit. I was once allowed to climb its single, straight, steep flight of stairs, like a ship's gangway, and by the time I got to the top I was giddy. Funnily enough, I often feel like that when I reach the pulpit and preach today.

At this church I heard some hymns I still love – 'When morning gilds the skies' was an especial favourite, and we really did try to 'cleave the skies with shouts of praise'. Another golden oldie, 'Pleasant are thy courts above', I remember singing for the first time on an early visit to St Paul's where Mr Davenport, the Times works manager whom we had adopted as Uncle Sam, played the organ. I did admire his efforts because, at a time when I was struggling to play tunes from an elementary book like Fairy Songs for Little Folk, he could 'play by ear', as they say. He could listen to any tune and then play it, even filling in the right harmonies. What a gift.

Those were the first two churches I remember, but as we got a bit older and it was felt that we should join a choir, where else should we turn but Henbury Church, a quarter of a mile up the road? I was seven when I was put forward as a chorister. There were no cassocks and surplices small enough for me, so

The choir of Henbury Church in 1948 with the Vicar, the Revd Glyn Jones

while a couple were being altered I had to trail up and down the aisle looking like Dopey (everyone's favourite dwarf) with my hands buried in sleeves and feet tripping over my skirts. At last, garments that fitted were provided, and with a few lessons on how to operate the studs that held our stiff collars and dicky bows, I was ready to take my permanent place.

Our choirmaster then was Frank Palmer, and the vicar the Revd Albert Edward Whittingham. We could muster ten or a dozen men and the same number of boys – no girls were permitted then, and I don't think they even offered. We had an official head choirboy; when I joined it was Derek Palmer, later a prefect when I went as an eight-year-old to King's School, so I held him in great awe and respect. He did do his best to help us, however. When I began to sing solos at carol services I once missed my cue in 'See amid the winter's snow'. I still maintain it was the fault of the tenors and basses, who had decided among themselves not to sing an intervening verse. However the organist, Charlie Palfreyman, sounded the note – and it went on sounding. He waited and I waited. Eventually, it was Derek, standing in the wings so to speak, who came to the rescue and sang the verse instead of me. I was mortified.

Notwithstanding this shame I eventually succeeded to the rank of head choirboy, after Ira Bradley and Eric Booth had their turn. This put me at the end of the front row nearest the congregation, where I could most easily be seen, and from where I could keep an eye on the Edward Brocklehursts of

Broken Cross school cloakroom, with its memories of postman's knock, is on the left. The loiterers are waiting for a Manchester bus. The central lamp standard and Worth's building with its clock have gone to make way for a big roundabout.

Henbury School – scene of many parties but now a private residence

Henbury Hall, who always sat in the front pew (with gate, like many others). Things like offertories are of absorbing interest to choirboys. We peered intently as the plate came round, and were never disappointed by the couple sitting there. Invariably one or two pound notes fluttered from their hands, and we gasped at such generosity. By comparison, our offering was but one penny.

Things jogged along in this fashion as the war got under way. We were jolted when Mr Whittingham left to be an army chaplain , and in his stead as priest in charge came William David Thomas. He was to have a profound influence on me, but again his words and his example were slow to take root. What I remember of these days, Sunday after Sunday, was the terrible cold at mattins because coke was in short supply, and as we sang at full blast the frozen breath came from our lips like so many locomotive safety valves. By contrast in the winter evenings I remember the long blue black-out curtains drawn, insulating us so it seemed from the dangers which for all we knew lurked outside.

But in summer – ah, on summer evenings the west door could be left open, and the setting sun poured in, and the huge tree outside – now cut down, alas – would stir in the light breeze and we could hear its murmurings inside. At will I can call this scene to mind, and it never fails to move me.

I had another interest in these early days because I was discovered to be a church organist! This had not occurred to me. I played the piano after a fashion at home, and then in Sunday School, and was permitted to accompany hymns on the harmonium in church on one Sunday afternoon per month for the children's service. This was not much in the way of training. But these were not normal times. Mr Palfreyman had departed to the forces. One of our choirmen, Sam Woodman, of the collar laundry in Old Park Lane, took over at the organ, but he needed his holidays. Who could take over from him? I could, I thought. It was reckoned that I should brush up my technique, and for this purpose was taken as a pupil by Wilfred Southwell, then organist at Trinity Methodist church, and on the splendid organ at this church I learned my new trade. When he was there I diligently played my studies. When he wasn't, I attempted a few songs in the style of the organists I had heard in Manchester cinemas.

Later, Mr Southwell moved to St George's Street Baptist Church, so that for my regular Sunday lunch-time lessons I had to go there instead. It is pleasant to think that I learned at the very keyboard where Winifred Weatherman, an old friend of my aunt's, later became the church's organist and stayed for many years. I also had a few lessons from Mr Edgar Gulliford, organist at St George's who also laboured to teach us metalwork at King's School. This was my introduction to St George's, 'home' church of my wife Sheila; later I was to return to it as curate.

Perhaps at the time I'm writing about, growing towards the teens, I had too many other diversions, but it seems to me that despite Mr Thomas's efforts I did not take the interest I should have done in the 'churchy' side of church. Some things did ring their little bell. I was always moved by the eventide prayer that God 'will lighten our darkness', and the harmonies of the hymns that sounded around me can still bring a lump to the throat. On the other hand, we choirboys were much occupied in breathing on our wooden music rests and playing noughts and crosses with our fingers, when we should have been listening to the sermons or the prayers. The only priest to whose sermons we looked forward at that time, I fear, was the Revd Charles Davies of Rainow who, we knew from occasional visits, was good for a few jokes and could make us laugh.

It is a lamentable thing for a priest to say, and I try to remember it when I talk about today's young people, but I fear that at this age church itself had not enough to offer. Sunday School was a different matter, but even this we enjoyed for the wrong reasons. We liked the friendships and the parties, but our Sunday religious sessions were a shambles.

Possibly (I seek excuses) we had tried too many Sunday Schools and had not yet settled down. We began at Christ Church, but the long walk into town offered too many temptations to our collection pennies – they were liable to vanish into the two or three sweet shops we found open. So it was back to Henbury, but which? The parish operated like a binary star system, revolving around two centres. There was Henbury school, down its little lane by the Blacksmith's. It was near the church, but there were not too many houses round about. Then there was Broken Cross school, a good distance away but in a more populated area. The answer to this problem could only be to hold Sunday School classes at both, but to alternate social gatherings between the two.

Thus, being nearer to our home, we started at Henbury. But all our friends lived in the opposite direction and went to Broken Cross, so after a while we did too. We did our best, honestly, but by the time we got to Mrs Kellett's class, at the age of 11 or 12, we were extremely rumbustious and disinclined to think of anything but our own fun and games. I still played the piano for hymns – had I not taken lessons from Mr Southwell? – but as I sat at the keyboard I was regularly assailed by pins jabbed into me by the nearest girls. In due course I retaliated. Magnify this behaviour by the number of youngsters in the class and you have some idea of the bedlam. I am deeply ashamed – but who am I to grumble now at our young people in church?

Bless them, the teachers and other helpers didn't seem to hold too much against us, and regularly – in alternate schools, of course – they laid on some splendid events to keep us amused and above all together. In the summer we had field treats – one year the big wall behind Broken Cross school was actually knocked through so we could get to the field behind, and then built up again afterwards. How's that for service!.

But best of all, and most memorable, were the magnificent parties at Christmas. War or no war, ample food was laid on for us – and its very generosity could bring problems in its train. One year (Broken Cross) I sat during the grace eyeing the food within my immediate reach, and was much attracted by a green jam tart. I had not seen many green tarts, and I decided that was for me. As soon as Mr Thomas finished his prayer out shot my hand. It had actually touched the pastry when I felt a smart rap on my head. 'Bread and butter first', a voice demanded. I was humiliated. Not only was I made to wait, but it was Mr Thomas, the Mr Thomas I idolised, who had treated me so shamefully. By the end of the party I had of course forgiven him. But as you see, I have not forgotten.

At another party (Henbury) we had just sat down at the long trestle table with our appetites akimbo when the young boy opposite me was sick (these things happen). In those days the kindly helpers were greatly concerned for the victims of such occurrences and there was much sympathetic mothering over the lad. It was decided that one of the helpers should escort him home to the safety of his family. It must have been a big disappointment to him, but I fancy he was cheered on his way by the sight of a large dish of trifle and a selection of cakes sent home with him to speed his recovery.

Food was not the only attraction on these occasions. Another delight was the prize-giving. Books were doled out for regular attendance, and I have some of them still – The School that Couldn't Sleep, The Wild Man of the West, and my brother's Goodbye Mr Chips. What pleasure they brought.

Finally at our parties, there was the entertainment, provided by ourselves of course. We worked in private on our 'turns', ready to stun our audiences. We sang and played the piano, recited and (one or two of us) danced. One year, with my friend Gerald Martin, we put on a conjuring display. All I can say is, it was a relief that nobody disappeared. On an earlier occasion, when Mr Whittingham was still with us, we were shown film of the Henbury rose queen crowning. The show was given, said a *Macclesfield Times* report, 'by Mr G W Wain who has a cine camera'. Mr Wain was a well-known Maccles-field solicitor and, with his family, a stalwart of the church. Among those who provided further entertainment at that year's party were Ira Bradley, Katherine Teasdale, Kathleen Lomas and Marjories Ashley. Oh, and inevitably, me.

Of all the entertainment, though, none to our minds could touch the games with which we always finished. And most delectable of these were spinning the plate and postman's knock. Looking back, I am amazed by the way the adults encouraged us in these sports. I can only think that all of us were much more innocent, and we were much more trusted. Can you imagine the situation

Inside the old St John's church in Statham Street, Macclesfield. Its second replacement has just been opened on the Weston estate.

nowadays if young-sters of 12 and 13 were locked together two by two in a dark-ened cubbyhole? But that is what happened to us, and while we may have emerged breathless we were, I am convinced, quite uncorrupted and in-deed would not have known what that word meant.

The object of both the games mentioned is, of course, to steal a kiss, preferably with your beloved of the moment. With the connivance of the adult helpers, it was possible in both games to cheat so that two kindred spirits were locked in to-gether. In the first game all the boys and girls are given a num-ber, supposedly se-cret. A plate is spun in the middle of the floor by, let us say, a boy (they were usually first) who calls out a number. The girl of that number then has a choice – if she wants a kiss she rushes to pick up the plate before it falls to the ground, and claims her reward. If she doesn't fancy the experience, she can be dilatory and let the plate finish spinning. That was a great insult. Into this system, as a further refinement, it was possible by secret signal to find the number of the partner you wanted.

The same opportunity for shady dealing is given in postman's knock. Whispered conversations around the room will soon disclose the number of

Traditional church activity – St Barnabas Guides lead a procession of witness on the Moss estate in 1949.

the object of your affection. You simply call that number, and bob's your uncle.

Both schools were, it seemed, ideally constructed for this activity. Both had entrances which incorporated dark and companionable cloakrooms, with stout doors which could be firmly closed on any would-be intruder. That at Henbury still exists and brings back warm memories whenever I pass it; the one at Broken Cross has vanished with the rest of the school.

Not that we really needed little rooms, companionable or otherwise. After one Sunday School session, perhaps unseasonably reminded of what cloakrooms were for, I was so far emboldened as to plant a kiss upon one young lady as we walked over the large expanse of Broken Cross. We were spotted by one of the friendly teachers, Emily Broadhurst. 'Paul', she upbraided me – 'and on a Sunday, too'. From this I felt that any other day would be all right.

The last of our Sunday School parties that I recall, and perhaps the greatest, was the victory party put on for 100 or so children of the parish in September 1945 to celebrate the end of the war. There we all are in the picture (see Chapter 9) mostly smiling but one or two of us scowling. We had the usual feast and, at night, as a special treat, a bonfire and fireworks display in a field at the corner of Anderton's Lane, now built on.

It was a grand note on which to end, for an end it was, though we none of us knew it at the time. With the war over Mr Whittingham would naturally want to return to his parish, and Mr Thomas left shortly after our party almost, it seemed, while our backs were turned, for I remember no formal farewells. He returned to the area as vicar of Bollington, but died comparatively young.

No sooner had Mr Whittingham returned in November than he announced that he too was departing. Here was a state of things, with both the vicar and his stand-in leaving with some speed. However, the next vicar, the Rev Glyn Jones from St Paul's, arrived in 1946 and restored stability and a sense of permanence, for he stayed more than 20 years and became rural dean and a canon of the church.

Under Mr Jones we growing Sunday School youngsters transferred to a thriving youth fellowship, and I continued in the choir though now with a deeper voice and, as befitted us men, without a collar and dicky bow. With Keith Willies I shared the cross-carrying duties (a great solace to a young man when girl friends are in the congregation). But shortly after that the links began to weaken. I fell prey to that malaise which takes so many young people from our churches at a critical age, and I wish I knew the answer to the problem.

But the lessons of those years were not lost. All the time, it now seems to me, I was being surrounded and emboldened by a faith which needed time to come to fruition in its own way. The seed was fed and watered most strongly, I believe, by my Mr Thomas, though as is so often the case I did not know what he had given me until he had gone, and I never thanked him.

But I remember him, and indeed all those from my grandmother to Canon Jones who by stealth worked on me like a field which needs care before it can yield any harvest at all. And most often I think about them when I hear the words of 'Hail gladdening light', the evening office hymn which we used to sing. The words and the music bring back to me the tranquil promise of those summer evenings in Henbury church, when the west doors were open, and the air was full of sunshine, and the world seemed at peace:

Now we are come to the sun's hour of rest.
The lights of evening round us shine.
We hymn the Father, Son and Holy Spirit divine.

7

In Sickness And In Health

On a family visit to Blackpool I had a sore throat, and there was some solicitous clucking around me. The next day (it must have been holiday time) we went to look at the pagodas at Alton Towers, and I not only had a sore throat but felt decidedly ill. The clucking turned to anxiety. The day after that I was confined to bed, a doctor was called and the clucking that turned to anxiety now turned to tearful despair as he diagnosed scarlet fever. Nowadays that might merit a couple of days off school, and that is all; then it was a serious and possibly fatal matter.

Ill as I was, I was in no position to understand the tears that were falling around the bed of a seven-year-old as the family were told I must go to the isolation hospital in Moss Lane. I did not know then that an aunt I never met, my mother's younger sister, Margery, had died of diphtheria in that same hospital also at the age of seven. So somewhat bewildered by all the upset I was wrapped in a red blanket, carried out to an ambulance and whisked away, leaving the house to the weepers and the fumigation man.

So at Moss Lane hospital, built in 1900 and with 84 beds, I duly arrived, and that was to be my home for the next seven weeks. The buildings are still there, largely unchanged from the outside at any rate – the two-storey nurses' home, the far block which was the diphtheria ward, and the middle section to which the fever sufferers were directed. The buildings now form Weston Park nursing home, but on my visits there I have sought out and found the very spot where my bed stood for those weeks of exile.

For isolation it certainly was. No outsiders could visit me. Now and then my mother was allowed to tap on the ward window from the outside and I, alerted to her visit, waved back. The staff were very kindly and soon a message route was worked out and in operation. A lady cleaner there knew another lady who worked at the *Times* and so knew my mother. Along this network I kept in contact. 'Your mother says, What do you want when you come out?' I answered: 'Tell her, a gun'. This was not because I was feeling suicidal; it was the only present I could think of at the time'. And later on: 'Your mother says your brother is going to Bournemouth for his holiday. Isn't that nice for him?' 'Grrrr.'

In the first days I have only vague recollections of injections in uncomfortable places, but after about a week I was sufficiently recovered to start feeling bored, and thereafter we inmates had to try to cheer each other up. The older residents passed on to the newcomers the words of a simple ditty, sung to the tune of 'I'll tell ma when I get home', or 'So early in the morning'...

Mother, mother take me home
From this isolation home.
I've been here a week or two,
Now I want to be with you.
Goodbye, Doctor Lawrie,
Goodbye matron too.
Goodbye all the nurses –
And the licorice powder too!

GLOSSARY: Dr J.H.W. Lawrie was the town's public health officer, the doctor in charge at the isolation hospital, and also involved with medical services to schools. Licorice powder was a potion whose cabbagey taste I can still bring to mind to this day. It was meant to keep young patients 'regular' – the major objective in the medicine of those days. But bearing in mind our youth, and the fact that we were incarcerated in bed, I should have thought that a nostrum with the opposite effect was really called for.

The infirmary. A supermarket now stands on its site

Incidentally, the 'regular' regime was practised with enthusiasm in our household, hence the vast quantities of Glauber salts which I was sent to purchase from time to time at Hadfields, and which were doled out by one of the two men in grey coats who presided there. Our medical kit at home provided also

PRICE ONE PENNY.

Second Annual Open-Air

MUSICAL FESTIVAL

In Aid of the MACCLESFIELD GENERAL INFIRMARY,

IN THE

Public Park, Prestbury Road

(Kindly lent by the Mayor and Corporation).

On SUNDAY, JULY 28th, 1895, to commence at 2.45 p.m. prompt.

Conductor: Dr. HAYDOCK.

Leader of the Orchestra: Mr. W. H. MACDONALD, L.C.V.   Organist: Mr. C. E. JAMES.

BAND AND CHORUS OF 400 PERFORMERS.

Treasurer: HIS WORSHIP THE MAYOR (Mr. Alderman Thos. Pickford).

SELECTIONS by the Combined Band of the 5th V.B.C.R. (by kind permission of Lt.-Col. Thorp),
and the MACCLESFIELD OLD BRASS BAND, assisted by the BOLLINGTON & POYN-
TON BRASS BANDS, under the Conductorship of Bandmaster J. Kelly, 5th V.B.C.R.

Committee:

Mr. John Bamford	Mr. John Hepple	Mr. Joseph Mottershead
Mr. Thos. Booth	Mr. Richard Hidderley	Mr. Thos. Potts
Mr. George Brown	Mr. James Kelly	Mr. Norman Watts
Mr. James Harrison	Mr. W. H. Macdonald	

Chairman: Mr. EDWIN MORETON.   Mr. HARRY JAMES, *Hon. Sec.*

Collections will be taken at each Entrance to the Park, and during the Festival.

BROWN & SON, PRINTERS, MILL STREET, MACCLESFIELD.

Glory days at the infirmary – a carriage turns in at the gates.

A fund-raising card from 1922 shows staff in the children's ward.

amounts of Bile Beans and, in case these stirred up the insides too much, there were soda mints to calm them down and restore the status quo. I wondered why we bothered to disturb it in the first place.

Well then, the days passed slowly at Moss Lane. About a fortnight before we were likely to be released a reunion of sorts was permitted with your loved ones. We were allowed to walk down the drive towards the gate (whose posts are still there, I see). My mother would approach from the other side, and we would both be halted with about ten yards between us. From this distance we would shout our endearments. The many Cold War television pictures of spies being exchanged on bridges always remind me most forcibly of these Moss Lane encounters.

Still, all was well in the end and home I went, cured and no more contagious. The gun awaited me; also a present from Bournemouth. As you can see, I had no complaints.

My only other hospital stay to date involved four days at the old Macclesfield Infirmary. After this time I left, but my tonsils didn't. I remember the primitive chloroform pad being applied despite my shouts, and I still recall the vivid dream of the sun chasing the moon as I went under. Afterwards, to speed my recovery, I was prescribed some ice-cream, though goodness knows where that came from in wartime. The children's ward where I was nursed has, of course, now been swept away with the rest of the infirmary, and roughly where my bed stood there is now the cheese counter in Sainsbury's supermarket. However, half a mile away the town has a spanking new and ever-expanding hospital. Bearing in mind that the old building had stood since 1872, and was bursting at the seams, I still think it has been a fair exchange.

Macclesfield had of course another major hospital, West Park, or 84 Prestbury Road as it was known, which was designed by the great Gilbert Scott. However, I am happy to say I had no dealings with it as a boy because it began life as a workhouse with around 500 inmates, and didn't start taking general patients until the end of 1939. Many are the heart-rending tales told of elderly destitute men, being escorted thither by their sons, sitting on a wall on the way to rest their old bones and saying: 'Remember, lad – one day your son will be bringing you here'.

With Parkside mental hospital, then the equivalent of a small town with all its own facilities, I had even less contact and in those secretive days we as boys had little idea of what went on there. We passed its walls and fences two or three times a day, but never thought of going inside. All I can remember is the sight of wounded servicemen, in uniforms of startling blue and with white shirts and red ties, walking in the roads nearby during the war

But back to matters of more immediate concern. Things were a bit more casual in days gone by, and the first port of call for many people when they had injuries or pains was the friendly neighbourhood chemist – Leach's, for example, in the Market Place. You could go in there, ask for the dispenser and to him display your wound or demonstrate your cough. He would then prescribe ointment or medicine as the case might be – no waiting, no forms to fill in, and generally a satisfactory outcome.

Dr J B Hughes

Sometimes you didn't even need advice – the malady and the treatment were equally obvious, and the chemist was there to keep you well stocked up against adversity. TCP antiseptic was a boon in our household, for example, largely because my grandfather used a cut-throat razor. He would emerge from the bathroom in the mornings with bits of toilet paper stuck over his cuts, and the sharp, nostalgic smell of TCP clinging about him.

One had to be suffering more seriously before one troubled the doctor, because he had to be paid either privately through his bills, or if you were on his 'panel' by a small regular payment. My first such encounter was with old Dr 'Jack' Hughes, who had a surgery in Roe Street, opposite the Parochial Hall. I have only a fleeting memory of our meeting, but it did result in me drinking a bottle of pink 'tonic' which he prescribed, and quite obviously I got better.

Our next doctor was Dr Sidney Clegg, who had a part-time appointment caring for the inmates of the workhouse while it was there. His general surgery was also in Roe Street, a dainty little house which still stands as part of the premises of Sutton Castings Ltd. Through more regular attendance here, because of the many mischances of boyhood, I have a clearer idea of what went on, especially in the waiting room. There were in those days no appointments. You simply turned up with your aches and pains, along with 20 or so other afflicted souls. On going in you counted how many were already waiting. Each time a patient disappeared upstairs to the consulting room, you knocked one off the total. When you reached nought, it was your turn next. There was a combined dispenser and receptionist in a little cubby hole at the back, but he or she popped a head round the door only if there were danger of a serious dispute as to whose turn it was. We were in the main a self-regulating body, policing the queue and standing up for each other's rights out of a sense of self-preservation.

It is interesting to note that Dr Clegg's old house in Victoria Road is still caring for the sick, for it is now Nuneham nursing home.

Schoolchildren had another medical resource in those days – the clinic at the corner of Great King Street and Bridge Street which once housed the grammar school and, now spruced up, is the Education Services office. Here I made my first acquaintance with the ogreish figure who was to blight a few of my days in the next few years – the dentist. I take you back now to the days of slowly, painfully grinding drills, vast needles, and rough and ready anaesthetics.

I was put off dentistry for a while (but not now) by an encounter with Mr Sheasby and his accomplice on this occasion, Dr Clegg. I faced, it was decided, a difficult extraction, and it was thought better that I faced it at home, so in they both trooped to my bedroom. The screams as the ether mask went over my face were reportedly heard in the next county (I think my mother exaggerated), but the job was done, leaving my mother the task of clearing up the 'operating theatre'.

On various occasions after that, with many fears and forebodings, I had to attend the surgeries of Mr Phillips in Prestbury Road, Mr Robinson in Park Lane, and Mr Newman in Roe Street. Perhaps I was looking for the painless dentist, but as I sat bolt upright in their leather chairs – as was then the custom – and saw the cord turning the drill grind agonisingly slowly over its pulleys, and felt the terrible rasping on the teeth, I came to think there was no such thing.

At least I was spared the agonies reported by older relatives who had to rely

Telephone 2678.

9 a.m.
2.30 p.m.
6 p.m.

Park Street,

Macclesfield.

The Exors of the late:

Maria Need

11. Langley.

To

Drs. Somerville, Proudfoot & Gillies,

Fees for Professional Attendance and Advice.

ending June 1930

£4 - 17 - 0

Settled

The doctor's bill in 1930 – fee £4 17s 0d, please.

on the 'tooth snatchers' when they were in pain. One such, with a reputation high in the circumstances, was the celebrated chemist and comforter Mr Bowers, of Mill Lane. Into his shop you went with your groans, and to save distressing the other customers he led you behind a screen. He was held in some wonder for his bedside manner – he would talk solicitously, and while the dreaded pliers out of sight moved ever closer he would ask you to point out the wayward tooth. On the pretext that he was examining it there would be a swift scuffle, the pliers went in and the tooth came out, and that was all there was to it. Oh, apart from the threepence or sixpence charged for this service.

Now no one has anything to fear from the dentist. You can lie down in the chair and go to sleep. As I write these very words I watch the clock inching towards the time when I have an appointment at the high technology surgery in Cumberland Street. I am, of course, not afraid, not afraid, not afraid...

Another figure in the medical world of my childhood was the district nurse. Around Henbury we were served by Nurse Leonard, who lived in Whirley

Road and bombed around the lanes in an Austin Eight. I don't remember her coming to our house, but she was much sought after by the ladies of the village and its surroundings.

One nurse, doubling also as a midwife was, a few years before my time, the subject of an interesting encounter with Dr Alexander Gillies. He was then a young man newly arrived in the town, though he stayed to become a respected and even patriarchal figure. Carrie Ashley, mother of my wife Sheila, had gone to visit Dr Gillies to discuss her first confinement. She took with her for support her mother-in-law. Dr Gillies asked which nurse she proposed to have and was told, Nurse Clarke. Dr Gillies pursed his lips. Perhaps he felt he knew something the patient didn't. 'I think', he said, 'that you should have Nurse Swindells and not Nurse Clarke'. Mother-in-law drew herself up. 'Nurse Clarke', she said, 'is my sister!'

The young doctor had come to town to join the practice of Dr Somerville and Dr Proudfoot in the house at the bottom of Park Street, which later became the Register Office. Bob Ashley, Sheila's father and later a familiar figure on Carswell's lorries, drove the doctors around in their car. But HIS father had driven for another practice in the days when doctors used ponies and traps.

One day Mr Ashley senior had a routine examination from his employer, and when the result came through he was called in to the consulting room. It had been found that he had heart trouble. The doctor gave him two years to live – and the sack. Eeeh, they were 'ard times in them days, right enough.

8

My Circle and Other Families

Nearly 1700 young people (at the last count) shared something with me, something that helped to root us firmly in the community of Macclesfield and which I believe, in its small way, helped to do some good. We were all members of the *Macclesfield Times* Children's Circle, run by Auntie Hilda who was my mother Ena. The name of every child who joined was written by her in a vast membership book, which still exists, page after page of names and addresses and birthdays, from Betty Alsop to Sheila Yoxall. These I browsed through from time to time when I was young, looking up friends and acquaintances, and those I didn't know I felt I should.

The weekly Children's Circle column in the *Times* was nothing if not ambitious. It contained usually an introductory letter, a little serial or story, and probably a poem all written by my mother and full of good humour and good thoughts, à la Enid Blyton. These were often built around the supposed activities of my brother and me, but using code names – he always figured as Tommy who got up to mischief – and it added to our excitement when we recognised ourselves and what we had done. Occasionally my father lent a hand with the writing, and there could also be an article by a contributor, so it was pretty substantial stuff altogether. One week there was even a Shakespearean contest.

Happy staff outside the old Macclesfield Times office in Queen Victoria Street in the 1930s. Ena Maybury is seen with Jack Henshall (left, advertising) and Harold Smith and George Hollinshead (reporters).

I hope all this was followed with some interest by our young readers but, as is the way of newspapers to this day, they were attracted also by other things. There were gifts for the members – always a metal lapel badge bearing the design illustrated at the head of the column. Pencils and rubbers were given away at the office — for the Coronation in 1937 there were also pencils with a crown on top. But undoubtedly the major attraction was the weekly section sending good wishes to members celebrating their birthdays, since we all like to see our names in print. Hence the necessity for the long list of 1700 names and dates, all of which had laboriously to be checked each week. There were no computers then to aid the task.

Here for example is the list for June 28 1935. Each entry gave the name and the date of the birthday, but not the age, of course. You will see that one is nearly a fortnight late — I presume it was missed on the first trawl through the pages of names. A 'jolly birthday greeting', it says, to:

Gweneth Wainwright, June 15; Minnie Hughes, 29; Brian Waite, 28; Rowland Hodge, 28; Jack King, 30; Arnold Worth, 29; Bernard Devine, July 1; John Eccles, 1; John Potts, 3; Victor Trueman, 4; Clarice Wootton, 4; Joan Day, 1; Joan Higginbotham, 1; Harold C Lonyon, 2; Charles Osborne, 3.

The 'chats with little people' might nowadays sound extremely patronising, but childhood and its simplicities were cherished then. Attitudes began to change with the war; a year or so after it ended the overt sentimentality had vanished from the column, which had become quite small anyway in the days of scarce newsprint. Further, the Children's Circle had become, more prosaically, the *Junior Times*. But I like to think that the spirit of the early days, the motto encouraging youngsters to remember that 'good deeds, like a circle,

SERVER, FRIDAY, JUNE 28, 1935.

---

he Children's Circle

OUR MOTTO

"Good deeds, like a circle,
should never end"

Chats with Little
People ·
conducted
by
Auntie Hilda

kiddies,
/ou read this, I suppose you'll
rned from your holidays and I
're all brown and happy.
week we're re-commencing the
ons. I'm sure you're all anxious
prize, and the only way is to
rying until you finally succeed.
for the "Circle" next Friday.
week we have an article by
K. Ottley—I suppose I should
Ottley, now that she has grown
older children will remember
des by Dorothy Ottley have
for so long in our "Circle" that

HAPPY
BIRTHDAYS

"A Jolly Birthday Greeting" from
"Auntie Hilda" to the following Circlers :
Gweneth Wainwright (15th).
Minnie Hughes (29th June).
Brian Waite (28th).
Rowland Hodge (28th).
Jack King (30th).
Arnold Worth (29th)

OUR SERIAL STORY

"THE SECRET SUBMARIN

Chapter 5.

"Perhaps we've come to the plac
liver found, not Lilliput, you kno'
other one," said Sandy. "Gosh, bu
fellow's as big as an elephant."
Tubby emerging from the store
heard the latter part of the sen
"Who's as big as an elephant? I
I'm rather a little overweight for m
but you can't say I'm as big as an –

The Children's Circle column in 1935, complete with badge, motto, birthdays and serial.

should never end', actually sounded a tiny but clear call for civility and co-operation and tolerance.

Those were the virtues fostered by the other circles to which we all belong, starting with the family circle. Here companionship, more or less harmonious, was urged upon us by circumstances. For one thing, there was no central heating, and it is hard to remember now the constant and huddled battle we fought in winter to keep warm. If you weren't matey, you froze.

We sat in a semi circle as close to the fire as possible, grown-ups in the central places of honour and the boys fitting in where we could. If you faced the fire, your legs burned and your back froze. If you sat with your back to the fire – at the table, for example – all of your parts froze. Whoever dared leave the room was told to shut the door before even reaching it. We longed to keep the fire blazing but feared the regularity with which it had to be topped up, since this meant a trip outside in strict rotation to the coal shed. In wartime you had to take such coal as the coalman could get – great lumps one month, slack the next. We had the Co-op, and I'm sure they did their best, but the uncertainty meant that you took with you to the shed a hammer in one hand to break up the coal, a torch in the other, and a shovel in a third hand if you should have one.

The struggle is obviously engraved on my mind, for whenever I hear the song, 'When you wish upon a star', I am whisked straight back more than 50 years to a winter gloaming, a wind peppered with flying snow moaning all around, and me standing at the shed door shovelling coal into a bucket for all I was worth. As you gather, we must just have seen the film Pinocchio, of which this is the theme song.

Another circumstance forcing our fellowship upon each other was the lack of any television, where now a family might have a set in each room so everyone can watch their own solitary programme. Then we had a large radiogram (from Hodgson's in the Market Place), no more than half a dozen scratchy records, and no inclination really to listen to anything beyond the news and such favourites as Monday night at Eight and of course ITMA. So we chatted, learned from each other, read, and made our models, all together.

In summer when there was no need to cling together for warmth we found we still had the habit, and remained a close little group.

Nor was this the end of our circles. We had friends, and were welcomed into their circles and even their friend's circles. Youngsters popped into each other's houses and took a place in the bosom of the family, so to speak. Parties were an especial joy. Each household seemed to have its own strength. Thus, at Mrs Willies's we united in songs around the piano, bawling such maudlin melodies as this which I have never sung since but have never forgotten:

We never speak as we pass by,
Although a tear bedims her eye.
I know she thinks of her past life,
When we were loving man and wife!

Mrs Higginson, I have it firmly fixed in my mind, took the palm for the delicacies of her table, which invariably featured at least one lemon blanc-mange rabbit. She also had the endearing way of calling us her sweetie-pies. Bob Hunter's parents usually tried to do something different, and it was at their party that we had a little filmshow with the help of a 9.5mm projector, worked by hand. As we had not seen television the appearance of a flickering image of Charlie Chaplin on your friend's living room wall was a great thrill.

There was quiet kindness also at the home of Leslie Martin, the top man at the Macclesfield Co-op (his official title was managing secretary) and his wife, when their son Gerald and I were friends. They took me into their family circle, and while Mrs Martin introduced me to the delights of cheese and soldiers of toast for tea, Mr Martin flattered me by discussing trade in general and the state of the Co-ops and the level of their 'divi' in particular.

All of these activities, it amazes me now to recollect, were male-only as far as the youngsters were concerned, and perhaps this led to the air of single-minded exuberance. The problems of mixed parties surfaced later. After one lively evening at a girl's home we were walking quietly (honestly!) back along

Coal for the family circle – wagons and a lorry being loaded at Macclesfield station yard just after the war

Chester Road, boys and girls of 16 and 17, when a bobby on a bike stopped us and demanded our identity cards. I always knew that tangling with the fair sex would lead to trouble.

Honorary membership of another cosy family came to us through the fact that my mother worked regularly at the *Times* office while we were still small and needing cosseting. A lady named Miss Hancock was therefore found to look after us during the day in her home at 9 Langford Street, convenient to Christ Church school, and thus we became on nodding terms, at any rate, with many of the families in the communal yard at the back.

Miss Hancock died soon after we started at the school, and her sister, Mrs Watkin at 13 Lyon Street, inherited us, giving us lunch each day. She collected the rents for all the first seven houses in the street, and so we got to know these families too and the astonishing fact that they paid 4s 6d each a week for their homes. Mrs Watkin, having a lean-to kitchen, paid 5s.

Here we spent many dinner times, racing home from school with anticipation for what we should find on the table. What a cook my mother had found for us! Mrs Watkin produced from her fireside oven the most memorable custard tarts and queen of puddings that one could wish. More astounding still, even to a young boy who wasn't expected to take much interest in these things, was the fact that they were produced with no modern aids at all. How did they do it? There were no dials to turn for accuracy, no fan-assisted ovens, no pinging timers, and really nothing more in the way of temperature controls than a poker to shift the damper and thus regulate the drawing power of the fire.

Mrs Watkin – it is a mark of the respectful affection of those days that I never did know her Christian name – had a son Clifford who managed the branch of Hepworth's, then on the left hand side of Mill Street almost opposite Woolworths. He too was drawn into the task of looking after us, providing us with our collections of cigarette cards and now and then taking us all out in his Morris Eight motor – a very sedate method of transport. One Sunday afternoon, being dedicated to his job as was the custom, we sailed forth in the car with Mrs Watkin to examine other Hepworth branches to see what they could teach him. The answer, we gathered, was: Not much. I think it was in Altrincham that he studied Hepworth's window and was horrified by what he saw. Do you know – I can feel his indignation still – they displayed one raincoat by wrapping it round a pillar holding up the ceiling! How could anyone judge its qualities when it looked like a tube?

Clifford was also the life and soul of the Christmas parties at Lyon Street, to which we were invited as honorary family members. What games we played, what fun and laughter echoed round the little cottage. Sometimes after

The happy circle. Three adjoining pubs in the Waters are the Bull and Gate, the Millstone, and the Nag's Head. Opposite them, just round the corner on the left, stands the Tavern.

these excesses we stayed the night, and once found in the morning that snow had gently fallen and the world outside was white.

But best of all with this little family I liked the autumn nights when we sat, the four of us, with our own thoughts and dreams as we gazed at the fire, listened to the radio (provided the accumulator had been charged at the nearest shop), sometimes played records on the wind-up gramophone, but mostly heard nothing but the gentle hissing of the gas and felt the warming comfort of its ebb and flow. We were secure. All was well.

Finally I turn to a circle with which I was not very tightly bound. You will perhaps feel surprised that, even in a book by a curate, there is little about pub circles. But the fact is that when I was a boy children were not supposed to go on to licensed premises, and in any case my family were not pub orientated. I once – and only once – sneaked a look inside the Cock Inn, outside whose doors I had so often waited for buses and charas, but it was then dark and dismal in the extreme. I found just one room, panelled in dark wood, and with no more than a couple of souls supping in silence. That was the way of taverns then; they were regarded as retreats for the serious business of drinking, and all else was diversion. This is not criticism – it was how the drinkers seemed to like it. It was in marked contrast to the light and airy and cheerful lounges we are used to today.

As village pubs used to be – the King's Head at Gurnet on the road to Sutton.

However, drinking even in those days could have its funny side. Sheila's father was a great one for walking in the country with his family, and naturally after his exertions he was ready for refreshment. One day, up in the hills near Gradbach, he called to mind the existence of the Eagle and Child pub and, it being near closing time, shepherded his little ones towards the goal as quickly as may be. With minutes to spare, as he thought, he reached its portals, crashed open the door without ceremony and asked anxiously: 'Am I too late?' The woman inside, who he now saw was eating dinner with her family, paused with the fork halfway to her mouth. 'Only 20 years too late', she said. All unknown, the Eagle and Child had long since given up its licence and become a private house.

It has to be said that when I did push the boat out on licensed premises, I did so in a big way. It happened in 1950 that the brewery giant Ind Coope took over the Macclesfield firm of Lonsdale and Adshead, a household name in the town. Their premises, which gave off a distinctive malty aroma, were on Park Green, and as a youngster on my bike I had followed their smoking steam lorries as they crawled up Park Street scattering glowing cinders on the road. Ind Coope were anxious to demonstrate that this local treasure was in good hands, and devised a public relations exercise to achieve this end. They invited a party of councillors and other local notables to spend a day as guests at their Burton brewery, and to make sure all this was recorded, added two local journalists to the party. By the perversity of fate it was I, by now a junior reporter but practically a non-drinker, who was marked down to represent the *Times*.

It was a jolly day. We spent some hours, it seemed, watching millions of bottles sweeping along conveyor belts and leaping into crates apparently of their own volition. I liked that, for such scenes fascinate me, and I'd rather watch a documentary on the manufacture and packing of chocolates, for example, than almost anything else on television except Coronation Street. Anyway, after this entertainment we all had an excellent lunch served not with the house brew but with copious supplies of wine. Then we heard a few speeches before piling back on to the coach in a happy haze. It changed my opinion of the licensed trade. My word, they CAN organise a booze-up in a brewery.

I also had to visit pubs on numerous occasions for professional reasons, the presentation of trophies, for example, and hence I picked up some idea of what went on there. At the Old Royal Oak at the bottom of Buxton Road I saw my first game of skittles, and at the Bate Hall in Chestergate witnessed the incredible feat of drinking a yard of ale. I saw piles of pennies pushed down all over the place, learned at least the vocabulary of cribbage (one for his knob!), and had to watch numerous domino matches as if I was rooted to the spot.

Then at country pubs – the Davenport Arms at Marton and another at Lower Withington – I explored the mysteries of the gooseberry show, where growers vied for prizes with berries as big as tomatoes but looking seasick. At my first show of this kind, however, it turned out that I was greener than the gooseberries. I reported the weights of the winning fruit not in grammes but in ounces, which would have made them as big as footballs.

These then are some of the major circles of which I was part. More will be found in other chapters of the book. The result of all this joining together, the linking of family and acquaintances in ever-increasing circles, is that most Macclesfield people of 20 years ago knew everybody else in the town, or at least knew a friend's friend or – as the saying goes – knew a cat that ran up their entry. Perhaps the same is still true today. I hope so, because it means that one of the attractions of the town, a feeling that we belong and know each other and draw pleasure from each other, is as potent as ever.

9

War In Short Trousers

Macclesfield's service men and women played the courageous, loyal and dedicated part expected of them in the Second World War. The honour in which their names and their conduct are held are apparent at any of the traditional remembrance services at the war memorial on Park Green, and the emotions of those who fought and of those who grieve are most moving to see.

However, there is no doubt that those who fought their war on the home front were not so sorely tested as the civilians in many other places, most noticeably in the big cities. Macclesfield was not regarded by the authorities as a town likely to face sustained physical attack, and that view proved to be right. There were no deliberate air raids, only a few jettisoned bombs or misdirected doodlebugs. The total number of fatalities attributed to enemy action was three.

The editor of the Macclesfield Times inspects the war. Alfred Hanson, who was with a party of local journalists visiting army units in France and Belgium in 1939/40, meets the men in charge.

Of course, the grown-ups at home suffered greatly from the stresses and strains of anxiety about their friends and relatives in the forces, and a more global anxiety about the outcome of the war which remained unclear until the final six months. They faced also the hardships and annoyances of rationing with the severe shortages of food and fuel and other necessities, and if they toiled in one of the many mills and factories devoted to war work they had to put in ferociously long hours.

However, these torments were not commonly suffered by the young people of the town. We had no clear idea of the peril which faced the nation; we took it for granted that Britain would win. And while there was never as much to eat as we would like we didn't starve thanks largely (in my experience) to the generosity of mothers and grandmothers and aunts, who saw to it that we had more than our share of goodies. Even in the darkest days I recall birthday and Sunday School parties with ample cake and blancmange rabbits and so on.

All this is by way of explanation and apology for the fact that war to the youngsters of my age – I was rising eight at its outbreak – was not entirely the grim and fear-ridden experience that might have been supposed. On the contrary, it had about it an air of excitement.

I do remember that on the morning of September 3, 1939, I breakfasted in sombre mood, but that was because I was taking my cue from the long faces of the grown-ups who explained that the Prime Minister was to broadcast at 11am and we might be at war soon after.

I didn't hear the broadcast because with my brother Philip I had to go off to my duties as a choirboy at Henbury church, where the service began at 10.40. I expected a messenger to rush in with news for the vicar at five past eleven, but no one came and I had to keep my excitement in check until I got back home and heard that war was indeed declared.

That afternoon I walked with my mother down Anderton's Lane in Henbury. As we passed the house known as Dandycock Hall (later Damson Cottage) I asked my mother what was going to happen, explaining that I was anxious because I had never lived through a war before. I think I expected that before the night was over enemy troops would have landed and there would be fighting in the Market Place.

Well, they didn't and there wasn't. It was to be a year before the German swastika and cross appeared in the market – and then they adorned nothing more menacing than an impotent Messerschmitt 109 fighter which had been shot down and was touring the country to boost morale. I queued with a large number of other boys and girls, and was rewarded by a ten-second session in the cockpit, handling the controls and dreaming.

We did have an early introduction to the air raid shelters which sprang up round the town and which the authorities thought we ought to sample so we

The Lincraft model kits which drew boys to the Wilmslow Model Aircraft Co in the war.

would be less frightened if they had to be used in anger. So with other juniors at Christ Church school I was shepherded across Great King Street by Miss Brough and Miss Whittaker and Miss Williamson and other teachers and led to the shelter on church land at the corner of Catherine Street. There in the gloom we sang a chorus of 'There'll always be an England' before going back to school. The psychology worked, and we were elated rather than frightened by the experience – after all, it was a break from classes.

Another occasion of great interest to the lads was the visit in 1941 of a couple of British tanks, one a Matilda and the other a Valentine. We straggled after them as they clattered along Congleton Road before turning into a field opposite the Rising Sun where they were to show their paces. My recollection is that they found the peaty ground not to their liking, and after watching them churning around aimlessly for a little while we all went home.

I suppose the fact is that nothing could replace aeroplanes in the affections of adventurous young boys, and it was in the RAF above all that we were interested. This enthusiasm was fed by the formation early in the war of the Henbury and Broken Cross Boys' Aero Club – a grand title for a youth group. It was the brainchild of two men – the Revd William David Thomas, by then priest in charge at Henbury in place of the vicar, the Revd A E Whittingham, who was on duty as an Army chaplain; and Mr W D (Bill) Scholes, who kept the little grocer's shop on Chelford Road, between Whirley Road and the Cross. The shop is still there.

The club was grand in its conception. It consisted of two squadrons, Fighter and Bomber, each with its squadron leader and lower ranks. Stirred by the activities of the local Home Guard we took to parading in the playground at Broken Cross school. On one diverting evening – obviously having seen a Commando film at one of the five local cinemas – we crept around Broken Cross with blackened faces to the feigned alarm of the few residents who were about.

Another highlight of our weekly meetings was the customary finale – a

List of Wardens' Posts in Macclesfield.

			Address.	Tel. No.
Wardens' H.Q.	....		Whiston Street	3664
Chief Warden	....		H. Sheasby	3666
Deputy Chief Warden..			W. F. Allen	3664

District.	Post No.			
1	H.Q.	1	Hermann's Office Cellars, King	
			Edward Street	3592
1		2	Castle Shoe Co., Waters Green	2491
1		3	10 Catherine Street	2592
	H.W.	....	H. Massey, 186 Peter Street	
2	H.Q.	1	Bruce Arms, Crompton Road	2546
2		2	43 Brown Street	2967
2		3	69 Park Lane	2414
	H.W.	....	W. Dakin, 213 Crompton Road.	
3	H.Q.	1	Pump Tree Farm, Gawsworth Road	3591
3		2	Catholic Boys' Club, Chester Road..	2812
3		3	"Elmhurst," Oxford Road	2628
	H.W.	....	L. H. Lomas, "Highbank,'" Whirley.	
4	H.Q.	1	Beech Lane Tavern	2625
4		2	Whitfield Mount, West Bank Road..	2063
4		3	Tytherington Hall Lodge	3597
	H.W.	....	A. Hughes, 6 Westbrook Drive.	
5	H.Q.	1	Hurdsfield House Basement	2382
5		2	160, Hurdsfield Road...............	2621
5		3	Welch's Stables, Fence Street	2603
	H.W.	....	A. E. Kay, "Park View," Fence Avenue,	
6	H.Q.	1	"Ellesmere," Buxton Road	2022
6		2	Dale Street Mill	2866
6		3	Co-op. Garage, Jodrell Street.......	2771
	H.W.	....	H. Goodwin, 2 Ecton Avenue.	
7	H.Q.	1	Brunswick Sunday School	2011
7		2	Seven Stars Cellars, Mill Lane	3593
7		3	Jackson's Stables, Byrons Lane	3598
	H.W.	....	N. Taylor, 77 Hobson Street.	
8		1	Highfield Coach House, Park Lane..	2970
8		2	Sunnybank Garage, London Road ..	2440
8		3	Moss Rose Mission House, Moss Lane	2632
8	H.Q.	4	Welfare Centre, Sanders Square, Moss	
			Estate	3800
	H.W.	....	H. Pearson, 95 Ryles Park Road.	

Macclesfield's leading air raid wardens and their posts.

ghost story told in the darkness by the resourceful Mr Thomas. He also entertained us from time to time with displays of water divining, while in summer we formed a cricket eleven and played, among others, King's School under fifteens and teams at Congleton and Marple.

Things became a little more purposeful later on when two of the older boys – Rex Carter and John Blackstone – started classes (with exams!) on aircraft recognition. We were also busily at work on a succession of model planes, made out of kits. Most of these we bought at our favourite toy shop – Tom Wood's in Mill Street – but occasionally we pedalled off to Wilmslow to visit the Model Aircraft Co in Water Lane, which marketed its own Lincraft kits. Presumably these were named after nearby Lindow.

These non-flying models were made out of solid wood – beginners chose

The fight is o'er, the battle won! Now it's time for the youngsters of Henbury and Broken Cross to celebrate. This is how they lined up outside Henbury School before the victory party began in September 1945.

balsa which was light and easily sanded to shape. However, we had among us some experts like Keith Skeggs who toiled for hours shaping hard woods, which made much better models. Our model-making endeavours were boosted on one occasion by the news that sheafs of model plans were available at the old Westminster Bank, near Leach's chemist shop in the Market Place. We rushed along and found that indeed they were being dished out – as part of a Wings for Victory Week promotion – by an elderly and rather puzzled bank clerk.

Occasionally our fascination for planes brought us into touch with disaster. Once while I was cycling home from school I heard that a plane had come down at Henbury. A hundred yards past our house I found it – a twin-engined Oxford trainer had crash-landed in a field and ended up in the hedge, only a yard or two from the lane leading to Henbury church. I take it this is the incident briefly referred to in his book by Terry Waite, who also lived in Henbury as

a very young boy. It is possible that the two of us gawped at this spectacle together.

However, the most poignant disaster, because it involved the local hero Syd Gleave, was the crash late in the war of a Lancaster bomber. Syd, a garage owner and TT rider, served as a test pilot at the Avro works at Woodford. On September 11, 1944, the plane he was testing went out of control and plunged more or less straight down into a field between Birtles and Over Alderley, instantly killing both Syd and his engineer Harry Barnes. This time, as the news spread, a regular convoy of boys cycled out to inspect the scene and its tragic wreckage which was still being picked over by police and aircraft experts. I can still remember the gateway from which we watched, stunned and silent.

This was my most dramatic memory of the war. Night after night I slept through the distant roar of the Manchester blitz, though I remember seeing the weaving pattern of searchlights on the horizon. I slept, too, through the solitary visit of a flying bomb, and I was furious next morning when my mother told me what I had missed.

Not that there was much we could have done about it had Hitler himself turned up at Broken Cross. The active role of boys in wartime was strictly limited, I found, to being something of a nuisance. We longed to join in such activities as there were, but the grown-ups had their own concerns. My grandfather for example, as well as being editor of the *Macclesfield Times*, was also the air raid warden for Henbury, and was issued with a stirrup pump with which my brother and I diligently practised. However, no one else used it partly because the metal sign telling the public it was available in emergency never did get fastened to the gate. And anyway, there never was an emergency.

The nearest I came to active service was my role as a bicycle messenger during a combined Civil Defence exercise organised for Broken Cross. Afterwards with the other lads I was allowed to attend the post mortem – how intriguing that title was – held in the empty shop next door to Dale's the newsagent. Here the grown-ups discussed the exercise's shortcomings and successes, of which we were blissfully unaware. All we knew was that we had had a splendid evening rushing around the lanes with our messages and feeling important.

How – at times – we envied the grown-ups who did seem to have the interesting jobs. My grandmother, for example, was one of many ladies who had the pleasure of meeting the foreign troops who were drafted to the district. This came about because she was in the WVS team who ran a canteen for them over Burton's in Mill Street (later the Savoy Cafe, and later still the Mykita ballroom). In this canteen, offering company and cheap food, congregated Dutch soldiers stationed at Congleton, Canadian troops and, of course, the GIs, many of whom were drafted into Macclesfield.

It may seem incredible but I can't remember ever speaking to an American soldier face to kneecap, despite the stories circulating among schoolchildren about their generosity with chewing gum and sweets. But I knew they were there, and they seemed to pop up in the most unexpected places. Once, travelling by train on the old Bollington line and reaching somewhere round Tytherington we were amazed and delighted to see in a field not only American servicemen and their tents but also a real plane on the ground, an Auster I think.

Like the ladies in the canteen, grown-ups spent a lot of time and effort trying to 'keep people's peckers up'. This was especially vital, of course, for the fighting men who were far away from home, and the number of cheering letters and cards, cigarettes and other gifts that were sent out to them, is incalculable. So is the good that they did. Here for example are some extracts from a letter sent about 1942 by a secretary named Eunice at Frost's mill on Park Green to Wilf Oakes, a colleague who was away in the Navy. I think it sounds a genuine note of concern and encouragement:

'We have had just the one air raid here on Barnaby Monday ... Fancy, only

Parkside Hospital had its very own fire brigade during the war. Here it is, ready for action, with Mr Sydney Barber at the wheel.

2 ozs of tea per week – Dad puts 2 ozs in one brew, so I don't know how we'll get on ... Neville Potts and Donald Dixon went into the Army last week. George hasn't gone yet and he is dying to get away ... There isn't much happening here at all; no excitement. I suppose you have plenty of excitement your way ... So glad you are coming home, if only for a few hours. Enclosed is a postal order for two shillings, which may come in'.

The real focus of the war, even for a boy living two miles away, was the Town Hall. Thither we were drawn – passing the mighty concrete tank traps installed at a strategic bend in Chester Road – at moments of crisis or emotion, just as Londoners flocked to Buckingham Palace. It was outside the Town Hall, for example, and visible for a hundred yards down Chestergate, that the giant indicators reporting progress in the various savings week appeals were installed.

These annual campaigns began modestly in 1940 with a simple thermometer being filled in as the town was asked to raise £5000 for a Spitfire fighter – a sum which today wouldn't buy the most modest saloon car. But the scope of the appeals and the effort put into them progressed mightily as the war with all its expense dragged on. There was Salute the Soldier week, for which a soldier's saluting arm pointed to the amount raised day by day. Finally the week raised £510,000. War Weapons Week contributed £750,000 and Wings for Victory week £530,000 – enough for 10 Lancaster bombers, 10 Spitfires and 10 Hurricanes. But most memorable for me was Warship Week in 1942, when a giant hoarding of a battleship displayed finally a grand total of £750,000. This was enough to buy a destroyer and eventually the town adopted *HMS Teazer*, for whose name we looked in all subsequent actions.

During these appeals crowds flocked to the Town Hall each evening at around 7 o'clock for what the adverts called 'The ceremony of the Indicator', at which a prominent figure would adjust the display to show the latest total towards the target. There were dark mutterings, as the week went on and the target was still not reached, that the authorities were 'keeping some back'. But if they were I congratulate them belatedly on their sound psychology. If the target had been reached on a Monday, and the fact announced, no one would have saved a penny more. As it happened, and just in time, we always raised the amount required, and that's what mattered.

Strangely, I didn't go to the Town Hall on the most obvious occasion, VE Day, when thousands swept into the Market Place to cheer and sing and dance and generally rejoice at victory in Europe. I meant to go, but I was too busy on the roof of our house tying a hastily made string of red, white and blue flags to the chimneypots. It seemed to me that I had helped to win the war; I should play a visible part in celebrating the victory.

10

Dinner Winners (and Some Losers)

Forget Michael Winner and his colleagues whose mission is to criticise cafes. I can suggest a better guide. There is no more reliable and influential judge of food prepared for the palate than a growing boy.

The boy has no loyalty to any particular establishment; he is not likely to be too much persuaded by the views of others. He simply follows his twitching nose and his taste buds to the meal of his dreams. If he is pleased with what he is served, he will return. If not, he won't. It is as simple as that.

I had the chance to put my independent assessments to the test when I went to King's School and discovered that at lunchtime I had the freedom of the town's cafes. We could of course stay for school dinners – and very tasty and well served they were by the resident staff. On one day a week there was a roast, carved by the master or prefect who presided at the head of each long table, but just as acceptable was another good standby, local butcher's sausage with beans and mash. Puddings were of the spotted dick and white sauce variety.

So we certainly would not have starved at school, but it was held to be a mite unadventurous to spend the entire 75-minute break on the premises. So, when the dinner bell sounded at 12.30, we were off like rockets. There was the sound of running feet pounding round the curve of the drive, across Cumberland Street, and into King Edward Road as far as King Edward Street, by Willie Wood's fruit warehouse. There the stream divided as each boy sped on towards his own particular feeding place.

My most favoured route took me down King Edward Street, along the Bate Hall passage into Chestergate and almost as far as the Market Place. On the left there stood what remained my favourite restaurant in all these years – the UCP. It is true that its outside was not too prepossessing, since it incorporated a shop wherein the local ladies queued for delicacies such as tripe and cowheel and trotters. But push through the revolving door at the left hand side and you entered something close to paradise – an oak panelled dining room full of tables each with its snowy white cloth laid for four people. Down here was usually full, or at any rate barred to us because of the chairs tipped up and reserved for grown-up regulars. So it was up the stairs, at the head of which stood a piano, and take your place please in the queue that invariably formed.

It was a wait well worthwhile for your 1s 7d (7 pence) purchased soup, a satisfying main course, and pudding. The cutlery was silver plate; so was the

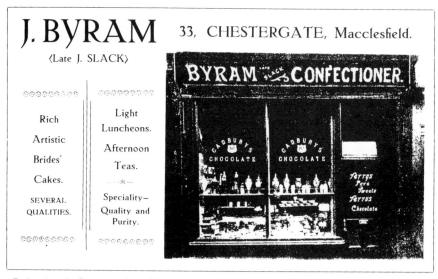

J. BYRAM   33, CHESTERGATE, Macclesfield.

⟨Late J. SLACK⟩

| Rich Artistic Brides' Cakes. SEVERAL QUALITIES. | Light Luncheons. Afternoon Teas. —*— Speciality— Quality and Purity. |

Early advert for Byram's cafe in Chestergate. Later, it expanded to provide a restaurant on the right.

tea service if you were a bit flush and added a drink to your bill. The waitresses in their black and white uniforms were charming. The only snag was that however hard we pounded we could not reach the restaurant before the choicest dishes – the roasts particularly – had run out owing to heavy demand and there were numerous scorings-out on the menu. After all, it was wartime. But never mind, that still left tasty meals like steak pudding or steak and cowheel, sometimes with chips if we were very lucky.

Another attraction at the UCP was the motherly manageress who watched over all her customers. She had also an elegant daughter who flitted in from time to time, and the rumour was that she was 'on the stage' and had understudied Gracie Fields, no less. The manageress's kindly ways could work to our disadvantage. My mother also ate at the UCP, usually downstairs in a regular spot by the pay desk. She was therefore in a position to be told that I – as often happened – had been in too much of a hurry for a full meal and had made do with soup and sweet. It was not easy in those days to get away with such behaviour.

Altogether the UCP, now alas departed from the town, was a place to savour. Later on, when I was working on the *Times*, I discovered that the editorial staff were inclined to judge the importance of a local wedding by several criteria, one of which was the venue for the reception. If the Macclesfield Arms was the top, the UCP alas came close to the bottom. I still think this unfair. Perhaps the tripe in the window could put a bride off, but the food and the surroundings

Whipped Cream Chocolate Sandwiches	Special Terms for Dance, Whist, etc. Committees	Pineapple Creams Wine Trifles, 5d. and 8d.

Byram's Café

Invalid Calves Foot Jelly	**Macclesfield**	Delicious Potted Beef and Chicken

were wholesome. As the writer of Proverbs might well have said had he been on the scene: better a UCP where good food is than a swish hotel and indigestion thereby.

Despite my attachment to the place I did from time to time sample other cafes in the town. One was Byrams, also in Chestergate, and we were lured in there by the tempting array of cakes and other goodies in the window. Their pineapple creams and wine trifles were much advertised and appreciated. Also, being a good bakery, it produced the most delightful rolls to have with our soup. Unfortunately, what is now called the ambience was not really suited to untidy schoolboys rushing in breathless; it was a genteel place, much patronised by the matrons of the town, and after a while we left it to them.

The same might be said of another cafe which attracted a better class of customer – Mary Etchells in Castle Street. This was an establishment I never entered unless I was accompanied by an adult. But her high standards were appreciated by many. About 1950 when the *Times* office had moved to Castle Street the editor, who was having important visitors, asked me to go down to Mary's and bring back seven cups of coffee. I did, and piled the cups on a tray. 'Saucers?' inquired Mary. 'No thanks', I said blithely, being myself quite prepared to rough it. 'We won't need those' But we did, and the editor smartly sent me back abashed to get them.

Some boys on the school dinner run swore by Pimlotts cafe near the top of

Mill Street – others swore at it. It was known to us, because of the look of the cakes in the window, as the 'burned offering shop', and truth to tell it seemed to cater for those who liked their pastries and other food, shall we say, well done. I hesitate to put it more strongly since the Pimlotts lived opposite to us at Henbury, and one should speak only good of one's neighbours.

In the Market Place was the Alexandra Cafe, which was not on our lunching list but which deserves a mention for another reason. One Christmas Henbury choir arranged its customary outing to the pantomime in Manchester on a Saturday afternoon, and down we all trooped, men and boys, to Hibel Road station. There we waited and waited while the mist turned to fog, and darkness descended prematurely, and we peered desperately for signs of the train. It never came, and great was our lamentation. We were told afterwards by someone who did get through that the comedian at the panto, as is the custom, made some joking reference to the choir from Henbury church, but we were not there and he spoke into a void. Perhaps he wondered why no one tittered.

However, in this emergency the adults in the party, and especially the choir secretary, Ernest Carter, were not to be defeated. There was a quick telephone call, and within half an hour all of us, a party of about twenty, had been shepherded up Hibel Road and Jordangate to the Alexandra Cafe, where at very short notice a table had been prepared for us and something like a party laid on. Thus was triumph snatched from the jaws of disappointment.

Finally in this canter through the cafes I turn with respect to Macclesfield's British Restaurant in the former Park Green Chapel – one of several such establishments promoted by the Government in wartime to offer cheap but nourishing meals. It was a bit more of an effort to get there, since it involved us running down Mill Street and along Park Green, and then back up Mill Street with full tummies. But the value was amazing, and I remember it well.

The system involved rushing in and buying tickets for your meal at a little desk, rather like going to the cinema. Thus equipped, you queued at the counter and handed over (I'm sure this is right, though it's hard to believe) a penny ticket for soup, a fourpenny one for your main course, and twopence for the sweet. A filling meal for sevenpence! The surroundings were a bit primitive, but the food was good. Later in the war, British Restaurant meals were shipped up to the King's School in insulated containers to save us the rush through town (we would have been a danger to traffic, had there been any). But on the whole the food seemed to lose its savour on the journey. Perhaps we missed the excitement of the chase.

Sometimes it happened that boys simply couldn't spare the time to sit down for a meal, and wanted to eat on the hoof, as has become the modern fashion. In that case there were ample facilities for them. There were at least four hot-pie shops within sniffing distance of the King's School – in Coare Street,

PARK GREEN, MACCLESFIELD.

Park Green in its wartime guise, with air raid shelters on the right. The old Park Green chapel, used as a British restaurant, is at the back on the left.

Brock Street, and round the corner in Beech Lane. Basically they were small grocers, happy to have the chance of an extra clientele, though whether in school holidays they were sad or relieved I wouldn't like to guess. In any case, few of their regular customers could have squeezed into the shops between 12.30 and 1.30.

What they offered were large juicy meat and potato pies or smaller meat pies, and these were 4d each. For desert there were teacakes at three-halfpence, but should we be too late and find all the teacakes gone, we had to make do with a penny flour bun, much stodgier and inferior.

And then, if we wanted to top the meal off with a drink, all we needed was one penny, and for this we could buy a Vantas. These drinks were available at shops which had installed the rather curious Vantas equipment, which looked like an inverted goldfish bowl filled with water and controlled by a pump handle. The shopkeeper poured an eggcup full of cordial into a glass, and then by manipulation of the pump filled it up with water from the goldfish bowl which, in its descent through the pipe, somehow acquired a supply of bubbles. The resulting drink was therefore quite fizzy. Various flavours were available. The daring – and the well-off – could pep things up a bit by requesting double or even treble quantities of cordial, but of course that cost them 2d or 3d. It was generally agreed among the commonality that such heavy drinkers were really only swanking.

One of the Vantas shops was in Brock Street, and I remember that quite well because, on coming out of it one day after imbibing a Vantas with me, one of my friends threw his house keys into the air in a fit of exhilaration and watched them plunge down a grid as neatly as a red ball potted by Hurricane Higgins. There were plainly some boys who couldn't hold their Vantas.

In addition to cafes and pie shops there were also available for our delight the snack bars of the town, although these didn't really come into full flow until after the war. At first there was just the Spa milk bar in Mill Street, a place of interest because of its array of percolators which bubbled with coffee, and Horlicks mixers. It had a back room with tables and chairs which came in very handy when we were visiting the Majestic cinema nearby. The Majestic too had a cafe, but the surroundings there always seemed a little too restrained for boys made giggly and boisterous by the antics of Abbott and Costello.

One of the first snack bars to open after the war was Mak Snacks, run by Councillor Fred Sherratt opposite the bus station. As it happened, the bar was next door to the North Western staff canteen, but I don't think the twain ever met. In those days of persistent rationing cafes and the like had to serve whatever they could get, and the Mak Snacks staff were at any rate innovative. You could get half a flour bun, thinly spread with butter and more thickly with a garish lemon curd. Or, more substantially, there were tinned steak sandwiches, which cost 6d – just $2\frac{1}{2}$ new pence, remember!

The operation was plainly successful because it was Councillor Sherratt, so we believed, who then launched out into another similar venture at the bottom end of Chestergate. This was Super Snacks, which drew much of its custom at night from patrons of the Picturedrome opposite, and Doug Bailey's dance hall down the street.

But the snack bar with which I became on terms of greatest intimacy was the Cavendish in Queen Victoria Street, because this was next door but one to the *Macclesfield Times* office where I worked more or less regularly from 1946 on. It was run by Mr and Mrs French. They became so used to seeing me around that in the end, when I wanted a snack of chips and egg and such like, they let me go down to the cellar kitchen and cook it myself. I was also allowed to pour tea for the customers when no one else happened to be around, and I consumed vast quantities of their speciality Kunzle cakes. .

There were other snack bars too at which my journalistic colleagues, from the rival *Macclesfield Courier* as well as the *Times*, met now and then to swap experiences. Useful for appointments at the bottom end of the town was the Fountain snack bar, paying tribute by its name to the nearby ornamental cast iron fountain which lamentably had been removed to aid the war effort. And

OPEN 9 a.m. till 10 p.m. daily. 10 a.m. till 10 p.m. Sundays.

Poplar Cafe & Milk Bar

65, PARK GREEN, MACCLESFIELD

Proprietor: A. W. HOLMES (ex-R.A.F. 1939-45)
in attendance at all times.

PARTIES CATERED FOR

Breakfasts   Dinners   Teas   Suppers

POPULAR LUNCHES—3-Course **1/7**
Daily from 12 to 2 p.m.
AFTERNOON TEAS from **1/-**
SUPPERS from **1/6,** including Tea, Bread and Butter.
Try our **POPULAR SUNDAY LUNCHES** **1/7**
Served from 12-30 to 2 p.m., and
SPECIAL TEA AND SUPPER MENUS

SOFT DRINKS, ICES, Etc.

Three-course lunches for 1s 7d – an advert from just after the war.

in Mill Lane there sprang up the Poplar Snack Bar, offering among other things suppers from 1s 6d including tea and bread and butter. Its advert promised that the proprietor, Mr A W Holmes, ex RAF, would be in attendance at all times.

So popular were snack bars in these austerity days that they sprang up in the most unexpected places – including Woolworths, who converted the counters across the bottom of their store into a serving counter. Their contribution to the drinking habits of the town was the provision of cups of coffee *made with condensed milk!* Rapture for a boy with a sweet tooth.

And as if all this were not enough there still remain for mention the long-established and everlastingly popular fish and chip shops of the town. No decent street was without at least one chippy, capable of filling one's stomach even in the darkest days of rationing. If by bad luck you couldn't get a fish – price fourpence – or even a penn'orth of chips (owing to a potato shortage) all was not lost. There were still shops – and I remember Balls in Hibel Road – which saved up the fried batter that had fallen off the frying fish and sold a bag of the pieces to hungry lads for a ha'penny.

We did have healthy appetites, and that is the only excuse I can muster for our often reprehensible behaviour in the shops. So eager were we for chips that we didn't stop to consider what hard work it was for the people behind the counter. First there was chopping up the chips, done of course by a device with a large handle that forced the potato through a square of sharpened plates. Large or tough potatoes would require a two-handed heave, and as the handle clunked down the earth shook. Then there was the messy business of shovelling coal or coke into the cooking range, for many had still not converted to gas. There was the constant risk of upsetting customers by not giving them enough, or trying to sneak into your portion a few of the coolish chips from a previous frying. And on top of all this there were rowdy lads keeping up a constant criticism and a stream of wisecracks.

Our local chippy in Broken Cross was run by Mrs Burgess in a shop just past Worths the plumbers. We were not kind to her. Our favourite trick was to wait until it was nearly closing time, fling open the door and shout: 'Have you got any chips left?' If, as usual, she said yes, then we would retort: 'Then you shouldn't have cooked so many'. And off we would run, giggling into the night.

What a way to treat a kindly, harassed lady who was struggling to stem our hunger. Belatedly, to her and to all who did such a good job at a time of food shortage, I offer a boy's apologies and thanks.

Park Green in its palmy days, complete with the famous fountain. This was commandeered in the war to build a battleship or two, but its name lived on for a time in the nearby Fountain snackbar of happy memory, and even today there are reports from time to time of some of the old ironwork being discovered in unlikely places. On the left is the diddly branch of the District Bank, a lovely little building noted for the tilework on its inside walls.

11

What's on at the Flicks?

For around 30 years, and especially during the war when we all needed brightening up, the cinema was the greatest and most popular of all possible entertainments. It's funny in a way that people went into a world of darkness to escape from the gloom outside, but I suppose we needed to turn the lights down on the real to focus on the make-believe on which alone, it seemed, we could rely.

So the great stars like Errol Flynn and Bette Davis and Bing Crosby peered out from the silver screens and brought romance where there was loneliness, adventure where so many knew only the humdrum, and glamour where outside was the ugliness of fear and shortage. Theirs was a world of magic, of transformation, and we in Macclesfield had so many passports to it – as every disbelieving youngster is told, we had five cinemas in the town.

The first thing to get clear about our cinemas is the matter of names and pronunciation – not that we were quite in the same confusion as Burnley. There the joke goes: Name three cinemas in the town that begin with the letters TH. And the answer is: th'Alhambra, th'Empire and th'Odeon. No, we weren't quite in that class. But we did have the picture house at the bottom of Buxton Road which in the twenties was the Super Cinema, in the thirties the New Cinema, and by the forties had become just The Cinema. In Chestergate there was the Picturedrome, never known as anything but the Drome. The Premier in Vincent Street was variously known as the Preemier or the Premmier. While the name of the Regal in Duke Street was always pronounced, mysteriously, the Bug Hut (and actually that started out as the Picture Palace). Only the Majestic in Mill Street, with its white tiled front and dome, had no pet or derogatory name, but the Majestic it remains to this day. Named like a Cunard liner it was certainly the pride of this little fleet when it was launched in 1922. And its sense of style was emphasised by the regular appearance in dinner jackets and bow ties of Mr Higginbotham, head of the company that owned all but the Regal, and the manager, Clarence Lovatt.

My apologies, incidentally, to those in Bollington who had their own Empire, but so insular were we that I never set foot in it, and now it's too late.

Altogether, then, with some of the cinemas changing their programme on Wednesdays, we could watch between eight and ten films every week if we had the time and the money – but both those commodities were in short supply so we didn't. In any case, we were almost always confined to our favourite

The Picturedrome,

Chestergate, Macclesfield.

Proprietors   -   -   -   -   -   -   Macclesfield Picturedrome, Ltd.
Manager   -   -   -   -   -   -   -   Mr. William Macready.

The Finest, Most Comfortable, and Up-to-date Theatre in Macclesfield and District.

CLEAN
COSY
COMFORTABLE

Continuous Performances 7·45 p.m. to 10·30 p.m.
(Saturdays and Holidays excepted.)

Saturdays and Holidays (Twice Nightly) 6.50 and 9.

Matinees   —   Wednesdays, Saturdays and Holidays
at 3 o'clock.

PEOPLES' POPULAR PRICES.

The Picturedrome in Chestergate soon after it opened in 1911. As you see, it was clean, cosy and comfortable.

cinema, which largely depended where you lived. We favoured the Drome, which was the first one you came to from Henbury, and the Majestic because it had the latest films. I think I went into the homely Cinema only once, and the Premier rarely, and the Regal not at all as a lad (but it came into its own as we got older, for it had double seats, you see).

How you took your film-viewing depended on the day of the week. In all the cinemas on Saturdays, and at the Majestic also on a couple of other nights, there were two separate houses, at 6.30 and 8.40. This involved some great logistical problems for the staff and the customers in those days of packed audiences, since to get one lot out, and the next in and settled in their seats in ten minutes, was no mean achievement. Sometimes at the Majestic, coming out at 8.30, we had a battle just to get down to the ground floor past the queues all pressing up the stairs to get in as quickly as possible.

If because of the queue or your own unpunctuality you were late and the programme had started, then you had to rely in the gloom on the usherette with her torch, and that involved a little battle of wills. SHE wanted to guide you into empty seats in the middle of a middle row: YOU wanted the back row, and an end seat if possible so you could get out easily when the film finished. We were not thinking of ourselves, of course, in this confrontation, but of the comfort of others. As we got older, and longed for a little head leaning on our shoulder, any folk behind you could get easily upset as their view was obscured. It was therefore better that couples should be at the back, but the girls with the torch didn't always see it that way.

Still, once we were in and settled, there was great anticipation as the programme got under way. It consisted of the feature film made up with shorts to last two hours. First to great cheers might be a cartoon, then the news, mostly about the war, and then if we were lucky a good magazine film like The March of Time. But a travelogue was likely to be greeted by jeers and catcalls. Then there were the trailers, 'Coming next week'. If every trailer were to be believed then Hollywood never made a rotten film, for they were skilfully edited – and still are – to give the impression that what was exciting for two minutes would be equally exciting for the full hour and a half. But a more reliable guide to the drawing power of the coming attraction was the phrase, 'Free list suspended'. Those who displayed posters giving the week's programmes received free tickets as a reward. If the cinema was going to be full anyway, the concession was withdrawn.

While all this was going on the atmosphere was building up in all sorts of ways. For one thing, smoking was rife and it was possible to see the beam of light from the projector lancing through a wreath of smoke. Occasionally there would be a sudden urgent scrabble and scramble for a burning dog-end which had fallen out of the ashtray and rolled under the seat in front. Then there was the rustle of crisp packets and sweet papers, and a fair bit of conversation if the short feature was failing to please.

But at last, after sitting through all these preliminary exercises, the film we had really come to see crept in upon us almost by the back door. The first we knew of its arrival was the projection on to the screen of the film censor's certificate. We strained to read the handwritten title thereon. If it was **the** film a great cheer went up, the titles rolled, and we were away in wonderland.

From time to time during the performance, but more rarely as technology improved, the projector would break down with a dispiriting whirr, and there would be darkness for a while as boos and slow handclapping began. But all that was required was patience, and in due course the film started up again very nearly where it had left off.

When the end of the big film was in sight – and with a weepie you could tell by the sobs, and with a war film by the crescendo of gunfire – then you had another fine decision to make. Hands up all those of you who worked it out correctly and managed to catch the last flicker of the film and still get outside before the National Anthem? Unpatriotic it may now sound, but there weren't too many at the younger end who stood to attention with enthusiasm. Not when it paid to be first in the chip-shop queue.

If much of this still sounds familiar to the cinema-goer of today, perhaps a mention of the prices will remind you that things were different. Even in the war years seats cost from 9d (4p) to 1s.9d (9p). The children's matinees on Saturday afternoon were even cheaper, a mere threepence to sixpence (depending on cinema).

Now whatever discomforts might have been felt at the regular shows, the matinees were state-of-the-art torture to the unlucky adults, but bliss to the youngsters. First there were the long queues to get in – and a certain amount of pushing and shoving was inevitable. Once past the ticket window there was a stampede to get inside and rush for your favourite seat. The noise was incredible, redoubled as the films got under way. I remember two strange serials from my days at the Drome. One was The Mark of Zorro, in which our hero inscribed his initial Z on the faces of his victims with the tip of a sword. This inspired many imitators, happily with nothing more lethal than an indelible pencil. The other serial which left its mark, so to speak, was one about a character called the Scorpion, who walked around in a crouch and with one arm over his face. This too led to the emergence from the Drome of an army of little Scorpions in short trousers all bumping into each other.

Westerns, too, were highly popular, with the Lone Ranger and Tonto way out in front. All this was glorious excitement, and considering the small outlay it was a bargain.

Talking of picture-going in the forties calls to mind an interesting enterprise launched by Derek Meakin, a reporter on the *Courier* then, a computer tycoon now. At that time cinemas were not open on a Sunday, but the law did permit clubs to show films. This led Derek to hire the Brocklehurst Memorial Hall on Sunday evenings and show feature films on a 16mm projector to a young audience who first had to become club members. An added attraction was the screening of a local newsreel under the banner of Maxonian Films. This depicted Macclesfield events. One I remember was a visit to Macclesfield cricket club, and there was our old friend Gil Manssuer, also a *Courier* reporter, smiling out at us from the screen.

I recall this club as a highly popular innovation, with a queue of lads forming on the pavement under a toilet window in their determination to get in. Friends rallied round to serve pop in the interval, and a good time was had by all while it lasted.

The Majestic, at this time and since, also had its hours of glory with live entertainment, professional as well as amateur. In the war there were special Sunday concerts to buck up our spirits – the comedienne Suzette Tari ('Red sails in the sunset') was one of the stars. At one of these concerts I received a much-valued lesson in showmanship. Partway through the bill the spotlight swung from the stage and picked out a young girl sitting not half a dozen seats from me in the balcony. The compere led us to believe that she was one of the victims of the Manchester blitz, and certainly she had a bandage round her

'PHONE 2412.

MAJESTIC

PICTURE HOUSE, MILL ST.

FREE CAR PARK
(Owners Risk)

Week commencing August 25th, 1941

PERSONAL APPEARANCE OF

DUGGIE WAKEFIELD

AND HIS GANG

Including

CHUCK O'NEIL

JACK BUTLER

BILLY NELSON

and

Full

Supporting

Company

of

30

Artistes.

TWO Distinct Performances Mon., Wed. & Sat. at 6-30 and 8-45.
Tues., Thurs. and Friday Once Nightly at 7-15.
MATINEES : Wednesday and Saturday at 2-15 p.m.

PROGRAMME ... Price TWOPENCE.

Duggie Wakefield and his gang – appearing at the Majestic in 1941

head. She was then invited to sing, and gave us 'You stepped out of a dream', in a very sweet voice. She was, of course, rapturously applauded. The unworthy thought came to me later: Would she have been so well received had she merely taken her place on the stage?

As well as Sunday concerts there were also week-long engagements. One of these, in 1941, starred Duggie Wakefield and his Gang. Gangs were very popular just then, with the Crazy Gang and Charlie Chester and his Gang and the Gang Show, to name but hundreds. Duggie – brother-in-law of Gracie Fields – appeared in sketches with Billie Nelson and Chuck O'Neil, as well as a crazy cabaret, with full supporting programme, as they say.

Another week's entertainment, just after the war, was a 'grand variety all-star concert' featuring the toothless wonder Frank Randle, a very popular, broad North Country comedian. He starred as a gormless soldier in a number of low-budget films with titles like 'Somewhere in England'. In the concerts he was backed up by George Pitts the impressionist, various musical acts and a couple of jugglers. The local conductor Dick Hankinson (later my choirmaster at Henbury) directed the Majestic Orchestra.

At Christmas the Majestic stage was the setting for week-long pantomimes with local stars. The one in 1945 was presented by Rhoda Dawson, the Bollington dancing teacher, with 'fifty performers and seven beautiful scenes'.

Characters.

(In order of their Appearance)

Morgiana (Cassim's Slave) -	- **Rhoda Dawson**
Cogia (Alibaba's Wife) -	- **Arthur Kirkham**
A Policeman- . -	- **George E. Floy**
Cassim (Alibaba's Brother) -	**Frank Brogden**
Zaida (Cassim's Wife) -	- **Frank Hallows**
Hamid (Alibaba's Son) -	- **Joan Southern**
Alibaba - - -	**Frank Faulkner**
Robber Chief - -	- **William Halliwell**
Wak-Wak (a Sergeant) -	- **Harry Pleeth**
Magician of the Cave -	- - **Gavarnie**
The Palace Cat -	- **Stanley F. Woodliffe**

ROBBERS.

Pilfering Peter - -	- Eric Whitehurst
Simon the Scrounger -	Walter H. Adler
Burglar Bill - -	Tom Cumberbirch
Thieving Theobald -	Frankie Woods
Crooked Charlie -	- - Jim Allan
Wilfred the Winner -	Albert Wrigley
Slippery Sam - -	- Syd Hartley
Petty Larceny - -	- Albert Snape

EASTERN GIRLS.

Betty Green, Joyce Baskerville, Irene Davies, June Higginbotham, Catherine Teasdale, Joyce Trueman, Hilda Bray, Doreen Goodwin.

JUVENILE DANCERS.

Shelagh Gibson, Margaret Worthington,) "A" Train
Nancy Sturgess, Pamela Steward.   ) Dancers.
Pat Press, Pat Wilson, Marjorie Hooper, Jean Chadwick, Sheila Smith, Betty Shatwell, Enid Shatwell, Hilda Shatwell, Sheila Oldfield, Margaret Leary, Kathleen Wood, Margaret Jansen, Jean Murphy, Bernice Allan.

Cast list from the programme for Rhoda Dawson's pantomime, The Forty Thieves, at the Majestic in 1945

The principal boy was Joan Southern, well-known in local amateur dramatic circles and Poppy Poopah in the sensational Rookery Nook, to which we shall come later. There was also a magician of the cave (since this was The Forty Thieves), and that part was taken appropriately enough by Gavarnie, a highly popular and effective local conjuror who was rumoured to be a bank manager. Who can forget the astonishment as he filled the big Majestic stage with paper flowers plucked from an empty cylinder?

Talking of pantomimes reminds me that perhaps the best-known local 'dame' was Billy Gallimore, the barber from Mill Street, who appeared to great laughter in such roles as an ugly sister in Cinderella. And *that* reminds me of a pretty nifty soft-shoe shuffle executed by a friend of mine outside Billy's salon. It was worth a place in a panto. This was at a time when haircuts, like everything else, were in short supply, and eight or ten boys, not to mention adults, could sometimes be found waiting their turn for a short back and sides. I had just reached the door of his shop and was about to join the queue when this friend, the much-envied owner of a motor-bike, rode up and stopped. 'Can you help me?' he called. Could I not! I raced to the pavement's edge and, at his direction, held on to the handlebars while he propped the bike on the kerb. 'Don't let go', he said, and I was still holding on as hard as I could when he nipped through the door and got in the queue before me.

What was that film starring George C Scott? "There's one born every minute?"

12

Goodbye Wizards, Hello Turn-ups

This chapter is something of a watershed. It marks one of those vital moments of change that you don't notice at the time. Only when you look back is it obvious that your world has rolled on and cannot roll back. The days of play have gone forever. Henceforth, there are important matters to contend with.

First then, the play. On lazy days the Wizard at Alderley Edge was a favourite haunt, in several senses. It was then a simple country pub, but we did not go there for the beer – they wouldn't let us in, though now and then we did get a penny glass of lemonade at the door. And we also made use of their amenities, including a two-seater closet round at the back which gave proceedings a certain air of chumminess. But the main attractions of the Wizard were twofold, and one of them was the row of slot machines outside.

These were not, of course, the flashing, thumping, gambling machines of today, but honest, low-tech and low cost entertainment. Top of our charts were the football and cricket games which cost two players a penny each. For this you got the services of two teams of tiny kicking or batting, swivelling or catching players, each wearing a daintily knitted shirt. These provided endless hours of fun and a lot of satisfaction – I was much more successful on the cricket machine than ever I was on the real playing field (see Chapter 14 for confirmation). By way of diversion there were also weighing machines, a dial that professed to tell your fortune, and a device that gave you a mild electric shock. That seemed a reasonable variety with which to beguile a sunny afternoon.

However, when the lure of the machines had run its course we turned to the second attraction of this enchanted place ... we went to hunt the Wizard. In a little dell, near the road but hidden by trees and undergrowth, we had stumbled upon a cave which we were told was Merlin's cave. There are, of course, many legends concerning strange goings-on at the Edge, but we knew nothing of these. All we knew was Merlin's cave, and that was enough to scare us in an interesting sort of way. I suppose all young people, from the fairy-tale age upwards, are eager enough to flirt with things unseen. Three or four of us, as choirboys, once persuaded Mr Hough the caretaker to lock us in the church at night for half an hour, but though we looked and listened very hard we neither saw nor heard anything untoward, and felt quite cheated. To help this investigation I once broached the subject to my great-aunt Sarah, a dear lady who lived in Bridge Street and went to the Spiritualist church, and she assured me

Alderley Edge and The Wizard

that in that house, in the very room where I was sitting at the time, she had seen and spoken to her long-dead husband. What else-could I believe when she was such an upright lady?

All these matters were reported to the ghost-hunting gang, and one day at dusk, hearing a rumour that Whirley Hall was haunted, we kept vigil there from the lane outside. We thought we saw a spooky figure, but it turned out to be a tarpaulin waving on the roof.

So by the time we had heard of Merlin we were longing to meet a spectral old chap with a beard. There were rumours that he was waiting to rouse King Arthur and his knights, who were resting nearby until England should need them in her peril. We practically turned Alderley Edge inside out trying to find him, or anything else of similar nature. This was in the days before the Edge and its woods had become public and popular, with crowds regularly saunter-ing around. In our time it was quiet, and strangely beckoning.

In these conditions we explored also the shafts and tunnels of the copper mines on both sides of the road, found another cave looking out over the Edge and penetrated its depths, along with many other cracks and fissures. We gave ourselves some nasty scares, as we feared we had lost our way in their inky depths and might never re-emerge. But of Wizards we found nothing, although judging by some of today's literature others continue to take the matter very

The woods behind The Wizard – strangely beckoning.

seriously – more seriously certainly than we did. Truth to tell, if there had been any self-respecting spirits there they would have fled in distaste from us as we blundered whooping through the chest-high ferns in the wood, or sent our cries echoing down the tunnels and round the rocky galleries. Perhaps the shades were not interested in satisfying the amused curiosity of little boys, and if that is the case then they adopted the right approach, for soon enough we lost interest and abandoned them to their sepulchral silence. Or it may be that elementals need to be seduced and not bludgeoned into appearance.

One more attempt was made to disturb the spirits, and we descended one afternoon on the wood at Gawsworth containing the tomb of that local worthy, Maggotty Johnson, also known as 'Lord Flame'. He was a court jester, poet and playwright, and an excellent violinist. He went to London to seek his fortune, mixed happily with the aristocracy and entertained them at their revels. He died, back in Gawsworth, in 1773 and at his express wish was buried in the grave in the wood which he had prepared for his servant, who died before him.

A fascinating character indeed, but as boys we knew nothing of him except that here he was, buried in the wood. Someone had told us he was buried standing up, so we peered through a crack in the brickwork to see if we could spot him. No good. So that was another place of possible interest struck off our list.

There was one more object of our veneration whom I should mention, and we had more luck with him because he never really existed, although we wished he had. This was the Saint, Leslie Charteris's rakish adventurer who was the hero of 20 novels by the time he came to our attention. How we enjoyed these books, and imagined ourselves accompanying Simon Templar on his clashes with the ungodly, his escapades with the police, and his discreet romances with young ladies. As this was wartime it was difficult to get hold of his books – or any new books – and it was John Higginson, the chief archivist of our unofficial branch of the Saint fan club, who lent most of them to his friends. For the rest we had to pay weekly visits to the circulating libraries in Mrs Dale's shop at the Cross, or Dorey's at the Toll Bar, to see if any had appeared on the shelves.

The search for the Saint also started me on a lifelong devotion to second-hand bookshops. There was one in Stanley Street at that time, under the name of Moseley, which I browsed through often, though I never did find a Saint book there. My only real success was a textbook on gynaecology which I bought for sixpence but with which I made little progress, since my mother ruled it indecent. But I never lost the habit of searching through rows of dusty books, and it has been suggested to me that a suitable resting place for my ashes, in due course, will be in an urn on a shelf in Oxfam.

Well, these were the days of high adventure and improbable romance, which all young people know and which they think will go on for ever. But they don't. The break comes, and one day you realise the corner has been turned. It isn't necessarily that you put aside for ever your childish enthusiasms – I still have half a dozen Saint books on the shelf – but you see them for what they are. They are part of your past, and you treasure them, sometimes with wry amusement. But there are more important things in the future.

Lads of my generation were quite fortunate because we knew precisely when this corner had been turned and the past left behind. To the girls in those days it was perhaps when they first wore lipstick. To the boys, it was when they first put on long trousers.

This will sound astonishing to the young gentlemen of today, who wear long trousers of one sort or another from the age of six months onwards. But then it was a decisive step forward, not to be attempted until the age of 11 or 12. In shorts, you were boys; in longs with turn-ups, you knew at any rate that you were going to be a man, however troublesome the journey might be. It was a transmogrification eagerly looked forward to. Parents were pestered for months before they gave the signal. In wartime there was an added complication because they not only had to give the signal, they also had to provide the clothing coupons.

But the day came for me to change from grub to butterfly, and my mother took me to Chestergate to visit the establishment of Mr Challenor the tailor.

Maggotty Johnson's grave at Gawsworth

After due deliberation, and counting of the coupons, he fitted me out with one suit, coloured dark blue with a thin red stripe; and one pair of grey trousers with a grey and black jacket, known in those days as a windcheater. So far so good. Now came the time for one's first appearance in 'longs'.

The suit first, I think. Best to be seen in my full glory, and on a reasonable occasion, too. So it was on a Sunday morning, on the way to church, that I first went forth in this strange new attire with covered-up knees. I called first for Denis Earlam, turning into his drive by the sandpit, and O the joy as he caught sight of my trousers and I of his face. Such surprised pleasure there was, a beaming smile that I can still see, as this older boy summed up a newcomer to the ranks of men-to-be. Thereafter, there were more smiles as we met adults on the way to church, and I self-consciously showed off my proclaimed maturity.

Another consideration to be weighed up when deciding on the date for 'longs' was the matter of school holidays. It was best to make the change when you were away from school, so that, by the time you were back with all your pals, you would have had time to get used to them. Then, by your confidence, you could make it appear that you had never worn anything else.

Well, that was how you changed. It not only altered your appearance; it also made you more conscious of what you were wearing, and a little bit more inclined to dress smartly in your own way. We had started King's School, of course, in our blue blazers and caps but, pleading the paucity of clothing coupons, we could now demand more freedom in what we wore. Hence, no one ever protested about my windcheater, though it hardly fitted the school rules, let alone me.

Of course, we were still subject to fad and fashion. Whenever I look at today's young people, and object inwardly to the craze for the aggressive-looking baseball caps worn indoors and out, for eating in and presumably sleeping in, I hark back to the day of the King's School boater. It's incomprehensible how these fashions start, and harder still to understand how they catch on. But one summer day one boy appeared at school in a straw boater, presumably purloined from his dad's wardrobe. In no time, the town was being scoured for boaters, and as luck would have it a cache was discovered at Black's in the Market Place, costing 4s 6d each. Next, the bursar at King's found in his store room a long-forgotten packet of blue and white ribbons actually designed for the rims of boaters. If he had known they were there, he would never have imagined that he could sell them. But he did.

Boaters bobbed up all round the town. They were even cycled in, but a snag was quickly discovered because they blew off in the breeze. Nothing daunted, one enterprising lad found he could hold his on with a bit of elastic threaded through the straw and hooked under the chin. So in this manner we cycled home, deaf to the ribald shouts of other and boater-less boys.

Then, as quickly as they had flourished, they died away again. As far as I know none reappeared after that summer. But I will never forget the enjoyment they brought us.

In those days of clothes shortage many stratagems had to be employed if you were to maintain some semblance of a wardrobe. Aunts and cousins knitted scarves and gloves and pullovers in strangely coloured wool (it was all they could get). Some even knitted socks with that incredible three-needle operation that left me lost in admiration. Not that I was entirely ignorant of these matters. With make-do-and-mend the order of the day, as we struggled to prolong the life of what clothes we had, my grandmother taught me to sew on buttons and to darn socks, giving me sixpence for each skill learned.

To lose a glove was a disaster; to mislay a scarf a catastrophe. There was a constant search for new sources of supply. My mother negotiated with a neighbour for two shirts, one for each of us, and they duly arrived. They were all right – creamy silky creations, as I recall – but the snag was that we knew whence they had come, and it would not do to let other boys see you in home-made clothes. So we were reluctant to wear them, and were most ungrateful.

Now shoes were another matter. Since these were unlikely to be home-made you could legitimately wear second-hand ones (or should that be second-foot?)

Re-Printed from the Macclesfield Guardian.

THE

LOST HEIR

OR, THE

DAYS OF THE STUARTS.

A TALE OF MACCLESFIELD

IN THE OLDEN TIME.

Written expressly for the MACCLESFIELD GUARDIAN.

ALL RIGHTS OF REPRODUCTION, ETC., RESERVED.

MACCLESFIELD :
Printed by CLARSON & BAKER, MILL STREET.
1874.

Treasure from the second-hand shelves – a novel set in old Macclesfield and no one would know the difference. So there was a brisk trade in these articles, and they were offered for sale in the small-ads of the local paper. One such advert took Philip and me to the home in Old Buxton Road of a Mrs Fazakerley – how the name rings out in my memory. We were not the only ones after these shoes, but my mother had the foresight to insist that we took along our own paper and string to wrap them with, for these items too were in short supply, and in those days it was impolite to carry unwrapped goods in the streets. Mrs Fazakerley was duly impressed, and we got the shoes.

I was less fortunate when, wishing to sharpen up my cricketing skills ready to play for England, I desired with all my heart a pair of cricketing boots, size four. Though the country was at that time producing many things in order to win the war, cricketing boots were not among them. I cajoled my long-suffering mother to search Macclesfield for some, and at Hills in Chestergate we located a pair of golfing shoes, which were white right enough and had studs on the soles. Would these do? My mother decided they must do for me, but I knew they would never do at Lord's and eventually found a second-hand pair to go with my second-hand cricketing pads.

Well, that is how I gave up shorts, and the garters that held up my knee socks, and other matters like ghosts and wizards that pertain to boyhood, and moved on to greater and more earnest matters. But still these whispers of yesterday come back to me, as they do to all of us, and I find them most comforting. It is only by looking back that we can measure the great and important distances we have travelled.

13

Read (nearly) all about it

The question of *how* I started in journalism is easy enough to answer, bearing in mind that my indulgent grandfather was an editor. But *why* I was launched on this career may be a bit more surprising: I wanted to leave school. I had vaguely been preparing for something in the scientific line, and I was in the science stream at King's. But in 1946, when I was 14, the prospect of some further years of study began to weigh heavily. I wanted, like many before or since, to be out in the world, doing something. How could this be arranged?

The answer came to me as I sat in the front seat of my grandfather's Standard 10 car as he drove us back from a family outing. On the glove shelf in front of me was my brother's shorthand primer. I picked it up and glanced through its pages, and something stirred. If he could do these squiggles, so could I. And if I did, wouldn't that make me a journalist more or less instantly, without further delay? I broached the matter there and then to my grandfather.

He was a kindly man and at this time – though we boys didn't know it – he was preparing to hand over at the *Times* and retire. He therefore did what he could. He prepared a formal deed of apprenticeship which should start when I left school. I was persuaded (against my better judgement) to stay long enough to take my school certificate, which would set me free in the middle of 1947. In the meantime, I could start work at the *Times* on Saturdays and in holiday weeks, and thus start earning the £1 a week specified for me in my indentures.

With this arrangement I was content, but I was not so satisfied with the blow which now fell upon me. Philip and I had assumed that, both being journalists, we would at some time in the future enter upon the inheritance prepared for us by our grandfather and take up the reins of the *Macclesfield Times* company. Even as we contemplated this outcome wheels were turning in other directions. The apprenticeship he had arranged for me turned out to be one of his last acts as head of the company, for we now learned that the great Kemsley newspaper chain, proprietors at that time of the *Sunday Times, Sunday Chronicle, Empire News, Daily Graphic, Daily Dispatch* and a string of provincial newspapers, had its eye on the *Macclesfield Times* and now took it into the group, nominally under the control of the bigger *Stockport Express*.

My grandfather retired at the end of 1946, and I went among others to his farewell do at the *Times* printing works. Here there were many speeches and presentations but also, as far as I was concerned, a personal sense of loss. Just

An editor's reward – Alfred Hanson aboard the *Queen Elizabeth* on his American trip in 1947.

as I was beginning my career my prop and stay had been taken from me. Who would now watch over me in so gentle a fashion?

Part of Kemsley's farewell to my grandfather took the form of a projected trip to America for him and my grandmother. This was really a kindly gesture, but it was justified by the fact that many silk-workers from the town had at the start of the century settled in Paterson, New Jersey, to help establish a silk industry there. If descendants of these settlers could be interviewed and photographed this would make good reading in the *Macclesfield Times*.

This expedition duly took place but – would you believe it? – for some reason my grandmother decided not to go and it was my brother Philip who enjoyed the great felicity of a transatlantic trip with my grandfather on the *Queen Elizabeth*.

Thus it was that as I began going regularly into the *Times* office the only representative of the family still on the premises was my mother in the office. With the reporters away during the war she and Jack Henshall, the advertising manager, had also rushed around covering such stories as they could, but they were now back full-time at their proper duties in the office. My new domain was in the reporters' little eyrie on the top floor. The two windows commanded views over large parts of the town whose doings I was now to help report. At these windows we stood, half a dozen of us, one morning soon after I joined and were able to see quite clearly, a mile away, what was left of the chimney of Backhouse and Coppock after its startling collapse in the night.

A place at these windows was, of course, the privilege of rank. At a table by one of them sat Philip Murray, the sub-editor, a careful and upright man with a strong sense of duty but quite steely when it came to correcting the mistakes made by his reporters, principally by me. He was one of several brothers who were devoted to Macclesfield Town FC and to angling. He had a distaste for bad language; the furthest I heard him go was his remark when he gazed at the rain tippling past his window and observed that it was 'pimply sissing down'.

Next to the other window stood a desk divided into four sections. The window seat was the prerogative of Harold 'Smudge' Smith, officially senior reporter whose work lay chiefly among the heavyweight stories of municipal affairs, and also the parish church. He went on to become the news editor of the *Macclesfield Express*, completing 50 years in local journalism during which, it was said, he never missed a Mayor's Sunday. When he retired in 1971 he received an official presentation from the Mayor, Alderman Mrs Lily Davenport.

Alongside him sat Cliff Rathbone, who was to become perhaps the best-known local reporter of his day through his interest in football (he reported Macclesfield's matches as Silkman) and the highways and byways of town and country. All the three senior reporters took their turn at writing the Stroller articles, a sort of journalistic Down your Way which interviewed people with strange hobbies, but Cliff eventually took it over and really 'strolled' all round the area. He wrote 'The Dane Valley Story' and 'The Goyt Valley Story', both published locally. He became editor of the *Macclesfield Express*, and after his retirement did great work for the town's talking newspaper. I once met him rushing round with tape-recorders which he installed in old people's homes so they could keep up with the news.

The third member of this reporting trinity was Harry Evans, just back from the Navy. He was a kindly soul, and did his best to cheer me up as I bemoaned my lot – as all young journalists do – over cups of tea in the Cavendish snack bar next door but one. He went on to edit the *Wilmslow Express* in the same group, and later the *Stockport Express*, winning fame at the time of the Stockport air disaster by rounding up his staff and publishing a special edition – a very enterprising thing for a local weekly to attempt.

That left one place on this big desk for the current junior reporter. There were two of them before I joined. The first was Bernard Cox, a livewire who achieved some place in the annals of the old office by one day inadvertently loosing a poker from the back window on the second floor. It hurtled down and through the glass roof of the lean-to where the office manager at that time, Miss Capper, was innocently brewing up and washing the pots in an old brown slopstone. It missed her. Bernard went on to become a well-known freelance journalist in Crewe.

When he departed my brother Philip took this last place, before he too left for the *Stockport Express*.

Overseeing the whole journalistic enterprise was Arthur J Wood, the editor appointed three years before to run the day-to-day newspaper operation. He came from the Stoke-on-Trent evening paper, and his cry of 'When I was on

Two of the Courier's bright young men, Derek Meakin (left) and Denis Johnson, at a post-war press ball in the Town Hall. With them are Marjorie Brough, who worked in the Times office, and Pauline Renshaw.

the Sentinel' came to echo round the office like an incantation as he strove to get things done as he wanted. He was a most capable journalist, a decisive commander, and an enthusiastic participant in the town's affairs, notably of the Rotary Club. He was able to pilot the *Times* through many changes. Strange though how our lives interlock. Three years after I left the *Times* I found myself on his beloved *Sentinel*.

These then were my colleagues who did all they could to help my career, which began in a rather faltering fashion. I was 14 when, on one of my part-time visits, I picked up the phone in the reporters' room because no one else was there and carefully took down the details of somebody's whist drive. Then I wrote a little paragraph in longhand, left it on Philip Murray's desk, and found it printed in that Thursday's paper. I was a journalist.

It soon transpired, however, that I suffered from a certain dreaminess (I blame it on too much tea) which resulted in my treading a well-worn path to Philip Murray's desk so he could point out my errors, and also to the office of the editor, who did the same thing rather more forcibly. I remember one black week when I wrote up a wedding from the form we asked all couples to fill in. A report of this ceremony, gushing with references to the lovely bride and the tasteful flower arrangements, duly appeared. Alas, I had not noticed that in their anxiety to please they had sent in the form a week early and the wedding had not taken place when the report appeared.

Mr Wood could see the way the wind was blowing when I failed to get any certificates for my shorthand squiggles. This was despite my weekly attendance at the classes run by Miss Phyllis Ryle (later Mrs Clegg) in a room attached to Park Street Chapel. In my defence I point out that for week after week I was the only boy in a class containing Alma and 29 other girls and it was not only shorthand outlines that I had on my mind.

So I didn't get any of the plum jobs that were going. I never once, in five years, covered a meeting of the town council, and only once reported one of Macclesfield's first-team soccer matches. This was despite the intensive efforts of Kemsley newspapers to train all their young reporters, and this involved a weekly visit to Kemsley House in Manchester or the College of Commerce there. On one of these visits my colleagues included a young reporter from Stockport who 'did a bit of running'. He ran so well he ended up as David Coleman of TV fame.

Many of our journalistic activities were shared with colleagues from the *Courier* which, despite its noble past and some notable scoops, was by this time decidedly weaker than the *Times*. Nevertheless, it had some fine journalists, led by Harry Hayes. A word much loved by reporters could have been coined for Harry – he really is the doyen of local journalists, a man so dedicated to his craft that in his eighties he is still reporting local affairs for various papers as I write these words. In 1992 he was presented by the town with a municipal plaque honouring his 70 years of journalistic service to the borough.

His chief man in the office at the *Courier* was Eric Dunkerley, sub-editor and chief reporter, and he had a team of often-changing but lively reporters. Among them were Denis Johnson, who went on to the *Guardian*; Monty Levy, whom I met some years later on the *News of the World*; the usually irrepressible Gil Manssuer; and Derek Meakin, an able reporter and also one with a head full of ideas. In those days when youth fellowships and youth activities generally were just coming to the fore it was Derek who suggested the town ought to have its own youth newspaper. No sooner said than the Vanguard was launched, price one penny and on sale in all newsagents.·

The basic flaw in this grand design was its surreptitious nature. We could not let our respective editors know that we were planning a rival publication. At the same time, unless we told people it was there we couldn't expect them to buy it. In this dilemma I took an advert for the Vanguard in the programme for a Macclesfield Town home match. I sat in the press box with Cliff Rathbone, secretly admiring my handiwork, when who should appear alongside me but Mr Wood. Consternation! In an agony I sat as he slowly turned the pages of his programme. How could he not see my advert giving my home address? He must know ... but he gave no sign of seeing it. I think, on reflection, he was being kind to me, and in any case he must have known he had no need to worry. The Vanguard lasted two editions, and then sank without trace.

All this time I have been speaking as if all journalists were writers but, of course, there is another important group among their ranks – the photographers. When I started on the *Times* we were well served by Harry Warters, who with his wife ran a picture framing, photography and household goods shop more or less where the new road now cuts through Chestergate. Both were very generous to young journalists. Later Harry was joined in the business of photographer by their son Eric, who had the much coveted luxury of riding his Velocette motorbike all of half a mile to school each day and keeping it in the masters' garage.

Eric was nothing if not intrepid. One night at a boxing match in the Drill Hall he climbed on to the side of the ring in order to get a close-up shot of the bout, as they do in Madison Square Garden. Alas, his flash bulb touched the ropes as he pressed the trigger and the bulb exploded, scattering glass over the ring and the boxers and halting the fight for a lengthy clean-up operation. Eric was banished from the hall and left, muttering. I can vouch for all this because I was sitting at the ringside at the reporters' table, writing in a notebook that had been flecked with blood from an earlier fight.

The sad end to this little story is that Eric, so much envied for his motorbike and his dashing style, died tragically young, leaving his parents shattered. Harry left the *Times* and his place was taken by Henry Redfern, from Congleton.

The *Courier*'s cameraman through these years was the cheerful Charlie Berrisford, whose shop was in Cross Street at the bottom of Byrons Lane. Charlie was a character; so was his little Austin Seven, which frequently took a full load of reporters and their girl friends on their assignments. On one memorable occasion, with five of us aboard, it once (and only just) puffed its way up the hill from Wincle to Clulow Cross.

In all this time I did have one moment of glory and strode into town between applauding crowds. Old readers will remember the name of Russell Wright, who took it into his head in 1951 to walk backwards to Buxton, all 12 hilly miles, to emulate a feat performed in 1902 by another local hero, John Alcock. To me was allotted the task of accompanying the enterprise for the *Times*, while Colin Mellor represented the *Courier*, and while Mr Wright sweated his way along the winding road we reporters travelled in luxury in my grandfather's Vauxhall which I had borrowed.

Then, bless me if Mr Wright didn't decide to do the walk backwards to

Every young person in
Macclesfield should read

THE
VANGUARD

(Youth Newspaper)

The first of only two editions of the
Vanguard, and the one and only advert
from a soccer programme.

Edited by Youth for Youth

Published every month—1d.

Order your copy now from your
newsagent   or   through   your
youth club.

Marena, Chelford Road, Henbury

No. 1   Vol. 1

**The
Vanguard**

Youth Newspaper
MONTHLY - - - 1d.

Monday Jan 10, 1949

OUR OPINION

It certainly amazed me a few
weeks ago when, at a public
gathering, an elderly, grey-haired
gentleman told his audience that
he disapproved of free milk and
school meals. He also advocated
that parents should have a
stricter check on their children's
activities, and he said that the
increase in juvenile crime was, in
his opinion, due to the lack of

Youth Ball flopped
-Mayor slates 'idlers'

CRITICISM AT COUNCIL MEETING

It was revealed at Thursday's meeting of
the Youth Council that a loss of more than
£30 had been sustained on the first annual
ball, held a week last
Wednesday.

**Julie wants to
be a ballerina**

Little Julie Wild, whose solo
dancing has captivated audiences
at the Christ Church panto, has
a pet ambition.

She told " Vanguard ": " When
I grow up I want to be a ballet
dancer."

Julie, aged 11, has been dancing

The Mayor, R. Wright
said that he thought
this was disgraceful. He
went on- 'As usual, a
few did all the donkey
work. I think it ought

Buxton and home again, and this time, owing to some contretemps, the local sportsmen he thought would accompany him decided not to. This was made clear at the start when there were Russell, and Colin, and me with my motorbike. You will agree that a guide is essential for a man walking backwards, and the main task fell upon Colin, who gamely set off. I roared ahead on the bike, and from time to time stopped to cheer them up. On the return journey I parked the bike finally in Buxton Road, and walked with the two heroes over the Waters and up the 108 steps between the cheering throng. I was modestly pleased with the reception. Oh, the return walk took exactly nine hours.

But such moments as these were few and far between, and the editor still felt I was a bit harum scarum for the job in hand. But isn't it strange? It is my duty to record the fact that Nemesis overtook Mr Wood in a spectacular fashion.

He did like a story with a bit of culture attached. So when one day he received a letter telling of the discovery on the Hollins of an ancient urn, possibly Roman, he was delighted. The letter spelled out the inscription on the urn, but none of us was a Latin scholar so it went in the paper as received, and a nice story it made.

On the day of publication all of us, including Mr Wood, were in the reporters' room going through the paper, as was customary, congratulating ourselves on a job well done. We came to the story of the urn, and wished we knew what the inscription said. Mr Wood must have had some inkling of disaster because he worried away at the problem like a terrier. We pondered, turning the phrase over in our collective minds and saying it aloud...

It was Clifford on whom the light dawned with a blinding and awful clarity. He blurted out the same sequence of letters indeed, but punctuated them differently, and thereby revealed their true meaning. It was not a motto in classical Latin, as we had supposed, but the description of a chamber-pot in rather crude Anglo Saxon.

It is no exaggeration to say that this reading was followed by at least ten seconds of stunned silence. It was broken by my nervous giggle, a young lad's unstoppable reaction to catastrophe on a scale he had never previously known. That giggle was the signal for Mr Wood to pound into action like an injured elephant. He ran down the stairs, sped to Smiths in the Market Place, removed from the counter all unsold copies of the *Times*, and called in the machine staff (sleeping peacefully after their labours) to print some hundreds of copies without the offending article.

He had done his best, but it was not enough to stop the sniggers. Worst of all, the address appended to the letter was alleged to be that of a mental institution in Manchester.

Heigh ho! Life goes on. Soon after that I moved on to seek a fortune elsewhere, and not long after that the town suffered a worse calamity because the *Courier* gave up its gallant fight and merged with the *Times* in the early fifties to become the *Times and Courier*, then the *County Express*, and later still the *Express Advertiser*. I wonder if the reporters today have as much fun as we had?

14

Those Sporting Types

I don't recall who we were playing, or what colours the teams wore. All I recall is that one goalie – ours – wore a green jersey and white shorts (or longs as they were then), while theirs had a green jersey and black shorts. Team strips in those days, as you see, did not display the same imaginative fashion flair as they do today. During the game our goalie – I think this was Williams – was injured making a daring save. The trainer rushed on with the simple bucket-and-sponge treatment, and after a suitable interval Williams recovered to the cheers due to a hero.

This incident on my first and only pre-war visit to the Moss Rose led me, young as I was, to two important decisions. One was that I must be a goalkeeper and earn the sympathetic applause of the crowd; the other was never to support a team wearing black shorts. This led me to some difficulties later when Macclesfield Town wore white and black before they became blue and white.

However, that is in the future and before we arrive there let us go back ... and back ... to the beginnings of Macclesfield Town football club

It came into being more than 100 years ago and at first played under the Rugby code. In 1874, however, when the club secretary was Walter Addy, it switched to soccer. Matches were played in the grounds of the Grammar School, in Bostron's Field near Coare Street, and for some years in Victoria Road. Giving these details in his 1925 book, *Fifty Years of Football*, the noted local historian John Earles lists the greatest players as William H Bolton, half-back, and the centre forward Bates, who played both cricket and football for Cheshire.

There was a notable victory in 1880 (Macclesfield 4 Burslem 0), a valiant draw in 1882 (Macclesfield 1 Stoke 1) and an amazing win in an 1883 Cheshire Cup tie (Macclesfield 10 Middlewich 2).

In 1884 William Bromley-Davenport first played for Macclesfield, against Chester in a Cheshire Cup tie at Victoria Road. A crowd of 1800 watched the home side trounce their opponents 10-1, six of the goals being scored by a brilliant Bromley-Davenport. He made such an impression on the sport that the *Courier* called him 'probably the finest centre-forward in the country' and he went on to play for England. He made such an impression in other circles that he ended up as Sir William Bromley-Davenport, of Capesthorne, Lord Lieutenant of the county.

There was more excitement in 1890 when Macclesfield met Nantwich in

MACCLESFIELD

1
R   Liddell   L

2   **3**
Harris   Prescott

4   **5**   **6**
Bardsley   Edwards   Daniels

7   **8**   **9**   **10**   **11**
James   Swindells   Lomax   Davies   Pool
(or Aldersay)

Referee: T. H. Briddon (Timp'y) ●   Kick-off 3 p.m.

Lewis   Jones   Frost   Smith   Powell
11   **10**   **9**   **8**   **7**

Thomas   Bates   Urmston
6   **5**   **4**

Morris   Parker
3   **2**

L   Hobson   R
1

SOUTH LIVERPOOL.

Alterations in the teams will be notified on the Board sent round the ground.

Edwards and Lomax were the stars of the Macclesfield team playing South Liverpool in February 1947.

the final of the Cheshire Cup at Northwich. Fifteen hundred fans travelled from Macclesfield, and had the satisfaction of seeing their team win 4-1. They returned to a heroes' welcome in the town.

In this period Macclesfield were credited with having some famous goalkeepers, including Jim Morton, Alby Smith and John Wilkinson.

In the 1890-91 season Macclesfield joined the Cheshire Combination, and at the end of that season moved from Victoria Road to a field next to the Moss Rose inn, where they have remained. They were champions of the combination in 1892, but two years later disaster struck when the players were told their wages were to be cut and went on strike for several weeks. Reserves kept the club going, but even Leek were able to beat this weakened side 5-1 before normal games were resumed, and in 1895 the team finished second to Everton in the combination.

That season, however, brought fresh disaster. The club became a limited company but went bankrupt amid some rather grand plans to develop the commercial potential of the ground. This became known as the 'Moss Rose Bubble'. The company was wound up, and shareholders got a silver sixpence for each £1 share. Valuable and talented players left, and it was years before the club recovered from the blow. They took to competing in the North Staffordshire league, and then in 1900 the Manchester League, of which they were champions in 1906 and 1909.

We are the champions!. The Macclesfield team (now in blue and white) which topped the Cheshire League in the 1952-53 season

Recovery was completed by a brilliant season in 1910-11 when the club reached the zenith of their success. They were the league champions, and won the Cheshire Cup, beating Chester in the final. After the first world war they joined the Cheshire League, and continued playing old rivals like Altrincham and Northwich. During these years the star players included the centre forward Harold Kelly (150 goals in six seasons) and the great Len Butt, who was to return to the Moss Rose on occasions after the war as manager of Mossley.

The outbreak of the second world war again closed the club, which brings me back more or less to the point where I began the chapter.

In the six years of the war I remember only one visit to the Moss Rose, and that was to watch a rugby match. This was staged to provide entertainment in dismal days, and the Henbury and Broken Cross gang were there in force. Being King's School boys we discovered suddenly an interest in rugby, and thought it would be a good thing to have our own Broken Cross rugby team. We could play, we reckoned, on the up-hill-and-down-dale terrain of our beloved recreation ground off Pexhill Road and, bumping into Derek Palmer among the crowd, we decided he should be our coach. He readily agreed knowing the one important proviso that would save him – the whole venture depended on us winning the match ball which was to be raffled after the game. We didn't, and that scuppered the grand plan. Good try, not converted.

Very soon after the war ended the soccer fans got restive and decided it was time to revive the club. The *Macclesfield Times*, with that keen supporter Philip Murray pushing in the background, took the initiative, stoked up the enthusiasm in its columns, and finally organised a public meeting in the Town Hall with my grandfather presiding. The occasion, I remember, sparkled with all the fervour of a revivalist rally. It was decided to float a new company to run the club, with shares at £1 each (both Philip and I had one, along with many hundreds of other supporters). My grandfather became chairman for a season while the enterprise got under way (being succeeded by A D Crowder) , and in 1946 there was football again at the Moss Rose. Macclesfield first team competed once again in the Cheshire League, and the reserves in the Manchester League (with such opponents as Tyldesley, whose name sticks in my memory). Re-equipping the teams was not without difficulties. In one programme the team secretary, Mr H Hall, had to appeal to the supporters to donate clothing coupons so that playing kit could be bought.

All of this activity I followed with interest, at first as a schoolboy, sidling in free under my grandfather's patronage, and then as a fledgling reporter. My usual duty on Saturday afternoons was to write brief reports for the *Times* on the reserves' games, and provide even briefer reports for the football final of the Manchester Evening Chronicle. This was our responsibility because that, too, was a Kemsley newspaper. Reports for the rival Manchester Evening News were sent off by the *Courier* reporter on duty.

Getting these reports to Manchester in time for them to be printed and available for reading in the town by about 6pm on Saturday night was a triumph of organisation on the part of the newspapers, and of great anxiety and energy on the part of the reporter. We had to phone over a short report of about 50 words bang on the stroke of half-time, and late scorers and the result at full time. We were barred from the one and only club phone, and had to dash to the public box on the corner of London Road opposite the ground AND rely on it being unoccupied.

It was all a bit nerve-wracking, but nothing like the difficulties encountered by Harry Hayes in his young days of journalism. As a lad he acted as runner for the reporter – and runner was the operative word. At that time the nearest public phone was in the Park Green post office, and Harry had to dash there and back on foot three or four times during the course of the game, taking reports and scorers to phone over at fixed times. Staff came to know when he was expected, and deterred any other potential customer from picking up the phone until he hoved puffing into view.

So great was my enthusiasm that I still turned up at the Moss Rose when the first team were at home and Cliff Rathbone was covering the match. Thus I came to know some of the great moments and the great debates. The

Who could resist such a picture of youthful endeavour? This is one of the King's School junior teams, probably the under-14s, around the end of the war, although one or two members seem to be missing. Philip Walker is sitting left of the master in charge, Mr Hargreaves, and Gil Manssuer is on the right at the front.

player-manager in these early seasons was Bill Edwards, a centre half of powerful physique who once scored a goal every bit as spectacular as the one that undid Arsenal goalkeeper David Seaman in that 1995 European match, seen by millions on television. Edwards took a free kick only a yard or two inside his opponents' half. He gave it the full boot and the goalkeeper watched it coming ... and coming ... until finally, still going like a rocket, it zoomed over his head and into the net. With my goalkeeping sympathies I felt for that chap.

Nevertheless, despite great shows of skill like this, there was a sharp debate at the time on the respective merits of Edwards and the reserve centre-half, McWilliams, the sort of argument that gives soccer its lasting appeal. To this day I expect there are those who will speak out for the superiority of one man or the other. My vote goes to Edwards.

Other delights in these postwar games were the irrepressible displays of goal poaching by the centre forward, Lomax, and the emergence of a really impressive trio on the left wing – Warren at left half, Lyons at inside left, and Speak as the winger. It was a joy to watch them.

My own ambitions still burned brightly as I watched these stars on the pitch, but what could I do? Not much. I did buy a royal blue goalkeeper's jersey from the new sports shop of Arthur Whiting, then in Brunswick Street and later in

Churchwallgate before settling in Chestergate. Goalkeepers in those days, you will recall, invariably had roll-neck collars that made them look like deep-sea fishermen. However, even the possession of this important item of equipment didn't make me a goalkeeper, and in the only organised soccer match in which I figured at this time I played at centre forward for Macclesfield journalists against the printers of the two papers. The match took place on the Windmill Street ground, and all I remember of the result is that I didn't score.

Incidentally, some 20 years later in London I was rash enough to appear for the *Daily Sketch* journalists against their printers. I was amazed at how unfit I was, and when after 15 minutes I was removed from the field by unanimous consent I was replaced by a young reporter who had been out on the razzle the previous night, had turned up late and was so hung-over he could hardly stand up straight. And STILL he was preferred to me.

By this time, of course, I had left Macclesfield, but I was still able to catch up with them on their two best-remembered days. On January 27, 1968, I was at Craven Cottage for the third round FA Cup-tie in which the Silkmen tackled a first division Fulham side that included three England players, Haynes, Clarke and Cohen. To the amazement of the 28,000 crowd it was Macclesfield who shot into the lead after two minutes when Taberner broke clear. Clarke equalised two minutes later but then Fidler lobbed one over the head of the Fulham goalkeeper and Macclesfield went into the interval 2-1 up.

Ten minutes after the interval Fulham were awarded a hotly disputed penalty and Clarke equalised again. In their turn Macclesfield were twice denied what seemed legitimate penalties, and finally Haynes and Gilroy scored to give the match to Fulham 4-2. But as Wellington said at Waterloo, it was a damned close-run thing, and many commentators thought Macclesfield deserved victory.

Finally, on May 2, 1970, I went to Wembley to see the Silkmen win the first FA Trophy with a 2-0 victory against Telford United, with goals by Lyons and Fidler. It was, of course, a most exciting occasion, especially as my brother Philip and I, both having journalist's cards, were able to get into the huge press box high above the stadium. There we met Cliff Rathbone, still reporting for the local paper. Thousands jammed the Market Place and Chestergate when the team brought the trophy home to Macclesfield.

That seems a suitably high note on which to end these soccer memories and turn to cricket, another sport I have followed from earliest days. Before the war, with friends, we strolled through the wide-open gates of the Victoria Road ground on Saturday afternoons, generally paid our way by moving chairs for the older spectators in the pavilion enclosure, and enjoyed the skill of Stan Bardsley, the wicket-keeper, and Herbert Wilson the professional. Boys being boys, it was hard to concentrate for three or four hours on one game, and it

Three of the King's School's cricketing heroes are in this Macclesfield team of the early fifties –
Freddie Millett, the captain, is in the centre; John Higginson stands second from the right and Gil
Mansswer is standing third from the left.

was sometimes a relief to stand on the forms on the western side and peer over
the iron fence at the Parkside ground, where play might be more interesting.

I had begun my playing career back in Christ Church days when teams of
us were escorted to the playing pitch at the corner of Crompton Road and
Cottage Street – it has only just been built on – and joined in games with a
composition ball. King's School was of course better equipped both in talent
and facilities, and in my days there I was helped by instruction and tips from
three players who turned out to be among Macclesfield's finest –
Freddie Millett, Gil Manssuer and John Higginson. John was cricket captain
of my house, Thornycroft, and I played one or two games under his guidance.
He went on to become King's cricket captain in 1947, and the same year played
his first game for Macclesfield under the captaincy of Stan Bardsley. He scored
58 not out in this first game, played for the club for the next 27 years, and
played also for Cheshire.

My second contact with an illustrious player came when as a very young
lad at King's I was chosen for a mixed-age eleven playing a match on the first
team pitch in front of school – a great thrill. I remember the opposing

Gil Manssuer at practice in the Macclesfield club nets

wicket-keeper praised me for keeping a straight bat, so I presume that was my only contribution to the match. The captain of our team was the great Freddie Millett, who with great distinction led the Macclesfield, Cheshire, and Minor Counties sides, and used to drive around town in a sports car in the style of Bergerac.

While I remained for some years an enthusiastic player, my trademark was abject failure. While first-class cricketers apparently fear that they will not get past the bogey score of 111, to my recollection I never made it past eight. Nor was my journalistic contribution to the game any more successful. If I was put down to cover Macclesfield's game on Saturday the editor expected me to be there, from first ball to last, whether the match was at Victoria Road or Burnage. This seemed to me a great waste of four or five hours when I could just as easily write up the proceedings from the scorebook and get the whole job done in quarter of an hour. To this end I learned to beat a path to the door of Len Walton, the club scorer who lived in Crown Street West. I think that in the end he realised he was doing my job for me, and a word to the editor resulted in me attending more games with clubs in the Lancashire and Cheshire League. Longsight and Levenshulme and Stalybridge stand like gravestones in my catalogue of rather boring Saturday afternoons. But then, what else should I have done with my time?

Now then, what other sports can I call to mind? Well, there was tennis, our future in that game being taken in hand by my grandmother at an early age. From badminton in the back garden we progressed to the tennis courts hired out by Mr Coleman at the corner of Andertons Lane, Henbury, and there on sunny afternoons we went from under-arm to over-arm serves, but not much further. There was also a court available at Mrs Nesbitt's bungalow at the Toll Bar in Broken Cross, and once we had learned not to scuff up the grass we also made appearances at Trinity tennis club, opposite the cricket ground and now buried beneath the houses of the Whitfields.

And then there was swimming, but not too much of it. At the cost of fourpence for admission we made acquaintance with the old baths in Davenport Street at an early age, when it was still considered vaguely indecent for people of both sexes to be seen together in nothing but bathing suits. Consequently there were, as you will remember, both a ladies bath (small and white tiled) and the bigger men's pool (blue and with a diving board). Mixed bathing was permitted in the big pool on one or two evenings a week. However, concessions were made in the case of young people, and it was in the ladies pool that I attempted my first struggling strokes. I did not like the water; I liked it even less after I had been pushed in at the deep end by a passing lad, and had to be rescued by Philip and Keith Willies.

Attempts were made to teach backward swimmers by pulling them through

Hero of the baths . . . Fred Bramhall, who was still swimming in competitions in his eighties, is seen right with fellow Macclesfield swimmer Don Lingard in 1931.

the water in a harness held up by a pole, but I was not alone in distrusting this apparatus. As a result of all this I never did learn to swim at the baths. Occasionally I went along with the lads, but spent most of my time in the little semi-circular bath at the end of the big pool, which could be filled with warm water. The powers that be obviously understood the temptations this presented to boys, and the top of the tap was removed once the bath had been filled in the mornings. Nevertheless, it was quite pleasant to lounge in here like lizards for an hour or so, watching your skin go soft and crinkly, and this was much to be preferred to plunging into the cool water of the pool.

I was involved in one drama at the baths, being present on a Wednesday night to report a gala at which a young girl got into difficulties. She was saved by the quick thinking of Fred Bramhall, that champion Macclesfield swimmer who was still competing in veterans' races all over the world when he was in his eighties. His collection of medals from these events was stupendous.

However, back to the rescue. A race for youngsters had just finished when it was noticed that one girl in the middle of the pool had stopped making progress, and indeed appeared to be sinking. Fred, standing at the side, rushed to the rescue and, without bothering to take off any clothes, plunged in, still wearing his smart blue suit. He brought the girl to the side, where she soon recovered. Fred was warmly cheered and the *Courier* reporter and I, sitting together in a little alcove at the end of the baths, made our excuses and left so

Members of Henbury and Broken Cross Youth Fellowship polish up their table tennis under the benign gaze of the Vicar, the Revd Glyn Jones, in 1948.

we could rush back to our offices – it being press night – and get a late story into the papers.

And finally, rugby. Considering the time that Len Harvey and other masters at King's spent trying to teach me the rudiments of the game, I have had only a nodding acquaintance with Macclesfield Rugby Club. I covered a couple of their matches when they played at Fallibroome, before they moved to Tytherington and then back to Fallibroome. One moment from these games still stands out in my mind – a dummy pass by a Bowdon player which was as good as anything I have seen later on television. He came thundering down the wing, made as if to pass inside, thus drawing the defence, and then in the same movement swept both arms with the ball high and round his head and carried on running to score a try.

It's moments like these that make watching sport worthwhile. What a pleasure it has been, in all these years, since I made that first visit to the Moss Rose ground.

15

Curtain Up – And Down

Macclesfield is a town with a long and distinguished history of amateur theatricals – witness now the much-acclaimed activities of the Macclesfield Amateur Dramatic Society with its regular shows playing to full houses in its own theatre in Lord Street.

However, I speak of the days when it was a much more widespread activity, when most churches and groups had at least a nodding acquaintance with Noel Coward and Ian Hay, and maybe once a year rang up the curtain on their stars for a night. For one thing, of course, there was no television to provide entertainment at the click of a switch. And then, for six crowded years, there was the war whose horrors needed to be drowned in whatever distractions native talent could provide.

For these brief years, then, there seemed never to be a time when our house was not learning its lines for a show, performing it, or recalling its disasters. The fact is, we were a stage-struck family with Gladys Cooper and Evelyn Laye high on our list of idols. Our own star performer was my grandmother, Florence Hanson, who specialised in what are now called cameo roles – comfortable servants, shrewish wives, that sort of thing. Like many Maccles-field amateurs she was now and then drafted in to play small parts with the several professional companies which came into town, tried hard to make a living, and went. Thus, in 1928 she was to be found at the Opera House in Catherine Street playing in The Sport of Kings, and in the thirties she appeared with Joseph Bloor's repertory company at the Stanley Hall in that old weepie The Passing of the Third Floor Back.

Another company that played at the Stanley Hall was the Castle Theatre run by Harry Hanson (no relation). Plays on their list included Gentleman Jim, and tickets from sixpence to one shilling and sixpence could be bought in advance at Phyllis Mottershead's cafe in Castle Street.

However, my grandmother's major effort in these years was devoted to the public performance of the plays written by my mother, Ena. She was not only Auntie Hilda of the *Macclesfield Times* Children's Circle, but she was also a dab-hand at short stories and verse. She wrote five full-length plays beginning with The Phipps in 1925, when she was 17, and this was produced at Christ Church School 'under the direction of Mrs A Hanson'. The cast included not only my mother and a young Rural District Council clerk named Walter Maybury (later to be my father) but also such local luminaries as Jack

MACCLESFIELD
SUNDAY SCHOOL.

A DRAMATIC & PHYSICAL CULTURE
ENTERTAINMENT

will be held in the above School

On Wednesday, December 1st, 1926.

Commencing at 7-30 p.m., in aid of School Funds.

Programme will include: Gymnastics, Tableaux, and Musical Exercises by Male and Female members of the Macclesfield Amateur Gymnastic Association.

Special Engagement of Miss Ena Hanson and Dramatic Company in her latest comedy success

"IRIS PATRICIA"

Scenery kindly lent by the Denville Stock Company, proprietors of the Macclesfield Opera House. Electrical effects by R. Marshall Carr, Mill Street. Music by Christ Church School Orchestra.

CHAIRMAN:
COUNCILLOR J. R. WHITE, J.P.

Come and bring your friends to see a First-class Entertainment.
Tickets 6d., 1/- & 1/6

to be obtained of the following : Miss G. M. Loose, 206, Bond Street; Mr. H. Bracegirdle, 38, Barton Street; Mr. T. Sellers, 26, Francis Street; Mr. T. Cooper, Newton Street; Mr. Ashness, Peel Street; Mr. Lomas, Large Sunday School; Mr. A. Hackney, 20, Barton Street ; and any member of the Large Sunday School.

"TIMES" PRINTING WORKS, MACCLESFIELD.

'Special Engagement' – Playbill for Iris Patricia in 1926.

IDAY, OCTOBER 6, 1933.

"LEADING LADY"

Play Of Stage Life

MACCLESFIELD AUTHOR

Two Nights' Presentation

FOR her fourth play, which was produced in Macclesfield for the first time on Wednesday evening at Christ Church School, Mrs. Ena Maybury has chosen the colourful theme of theatrical life and has written it round a "Leading Lady" from whom the play takes its title.

Mrs. Maybury, who is daughter of Mr. Alfred Hanson, Editor of the "Macclesfield Times," and herself a member of the literary staff of this journal, could scarcely have selected a better subject, for the stage has more than an ordinary appeal to most people and the lives of its

First night review of Leading Lady in 1933

Hidderley, of Ray's mineral waters and later Mayor of the town; Billy Gallimore the barber from Mill Street; and John Fytton who won renown not only as an actor but also as a lay preacher at Christ Church.

Iris Patricia followed in 1926 and, after its premiere in Christ Church it was, in the best theatrical tradition, taken 'on tour'. A poster for the Large Sunday School announced the 'special engagement of Miss Ena Hanson and dramatic company in her latest comedy success'. Scenery was kindly lent by the Denville Stock Company, who ran the Opera House. This was followed in 1928 by Specimens, in 1933 by Leading Lady and then, in 1938 by The Question Is ('Her best play yet' – *Macclesfield Times*), which I remember being taken to see upstairs in Christ Church school.

The cast this time included Wilfred Biddulph, who later went on the professional stage, and Mabel and Alice Moseley, while a laudatory speech was made by the vicar, Sydney Sharples. For the first time (but not the last) John Fytton took over as producer, and the play was 'presented by the Central School Old Boys' Dramatic Society', which had been founded in 1929.

The society's lengthy title was one with which I became familiar in the next 10 years as we enjoyed our finest hours. I use the word 'we' because from then on, wherever my grandmother went in connection with the society's affairs, it seemed that my brother Philip and I followed in her footsteps like two little understudies. Our role was to help, in the Just William sense of the word. So we held up the scene painters, experimented with the grease-paint, and were to be found wandering around backstage during the performance.

The highlight, so to speak, of our assistance came during a performance at Newtown Methodist Church, to which the society migrated during the war with productions like Tons of Money and Nothing but the Truth. On one

Christ Church Ladies' Guild

In aid of the Roof Fund a
Play in 3-acts

"The QUESTION IS"

(By ENA MAYBURY)

will be given in

CHRIST CHURCH SCHOOL

on

Wednesday, January 26th,

1938.

PROGRAMME - TWO-PENCE

"Times" Printing Works, Macclesfield   Tel. 3125-6 (two lines)

Helping the Roof Fund: a programme from 1938.

occasion, as the curtain went up for the second act the lights went down, and then out altogether. As if by a magnet I was drawn to a little cave under the stage, which contained the electrics, and peered entranced through the torch-lit gloom at two sweating figures struggling to mend the fuses. After ignoring a couple of my well-meant questions they told me to clear off (I think I heard correctly). Shortly afterwards the lights returned, but I realised that my career as a helper was at an end.

However, I did manage to tread the boards on my own account. With a dozen other lads from Henbury and Broken Cross, including Keith Willis, John Higginson and Ira Bradley, I joined in a concert at Broken Cross Methodist church hall in the early forties. This was the result of a collaboration between

When every church could produce a concert party. This is a production at St Barnabas in 1946 with the vicar, the Revd J.W. Cooke, fourth from the left.

the Revd David Thomas, priest in charge at Henbury during the war, and my mother, and it was treated with the utmost seriousness. Tickets and programmes were printed, and you can't get much more serious than that.

Between them the two grown-ups organised the entertainment, putting us through rigorous rehearsals. There was one slight breeze. Because the sketches were written by my mother I naturally thought that they should be performed by my brother and me, but the other boys had different ideas and in the end the starring roles in such smash-hit sketches as 'Dr Glusoe' and 'Not the type' were shared round.

Once that was sorted out we learned to act, cavort, recite and sing (to John's ukulele accompaniment) to the very best of our ability. Choruses of 'Cowboy', 'Forget-me-not-lane' and 'Tan Tan Tivvy' still trip through my mind. We even had a guest artiste – Kenneth Turpin, playing the xylophone. Happily, the great night went off resoundingly well, raised all of £8 for the war comforts fund, and earned itself no fewer than nine column inches of praise in the *Macclesfield Times*. This write-up, including even a kindly mention for Norman Downing 'in charge of the curtains', may seem extravagant for a boys' concert. But then, you must remember that my mother wrote the report as well as the sketches, and my grandfather edited the paper.

This concert set me on a mini career as an entertainer. Under the guidance of Winifred Bracegirdle, who taught the piano and sang and lived near me in

Chelford Road, I sang with another little group who toured the halls. One performance, I remember, took place at the old infirmary. In the women's ward there, I hopped upon a chair and sang 'Bless this house', with Leonard Lee at the piano. My co-star was a young lady named Brenda Knight, who sang and danced. To such effect, indeed, that I can still remember her costume, the steps of her dance and the words of the song:

Salome, Salome, you should see Salome –
Dancing there with her feet all bare,
Every little wiggle makes the boys all stare!
Salome, Salome, you should see Salome –
Curtain rings stuck through her nose
And bells upon her dainty little toes.
She swings it, she flings it,
And the sheikhs all murmur 'Oh!'
While the old sphinx winks
And winks and winks
Out there where the sandbags grow!

This little party also included Mildred Steele, whom I remember for her very sweet voice – but perhaps that was calf love on my part. Among our other appearances was a show at the Town Mission (minus the Salome dance), and another outing to the Broken Cross Methodist hall. There to my embarrassment I was required to wear pyjamas and join in a stomach-turning rendition of 'Christopher Robin is saying his prayers'. As the curtain went up on this scene I espied in the front row all my least-favourite lads. I thought they would line up to throw the fruit, but perhaps they were as stunned as I was.

Returning to the story of the great fuse at Newtown, I recall that one of the harassed gents who sent me on my way was Alfred Wilson, who became a leading figure in the Central School society during the war while John Fytton and others were away in the Forces. Another leading light was Frank Snelson, the butcher from Old Park Lane, who established a reputation as 'Macclesfield's merriest master of mirth' for his hilarious portrayals in some roaring farces. My favourite, as a young boy at this time, was Rookery Nook because part of the comedy stemmed from the appearance of a young lady in her underwear. This character, as I have already revealed, rejoiced in the name of Poppy Poopah. Happy days!

The end of the war brought, if anything, even greater interest in the amateur stage. Christ Church and St George's both had operatic societies – who among those who saw the latter's Iolanthe will forget the stately fairies portrayed by Dora Orme and her colleagues?. The society could also boast, in its next production of The Yeomen of the Guard, a notable performance by Peter Robinson, who later won the Mario Lanza singing competition and went on

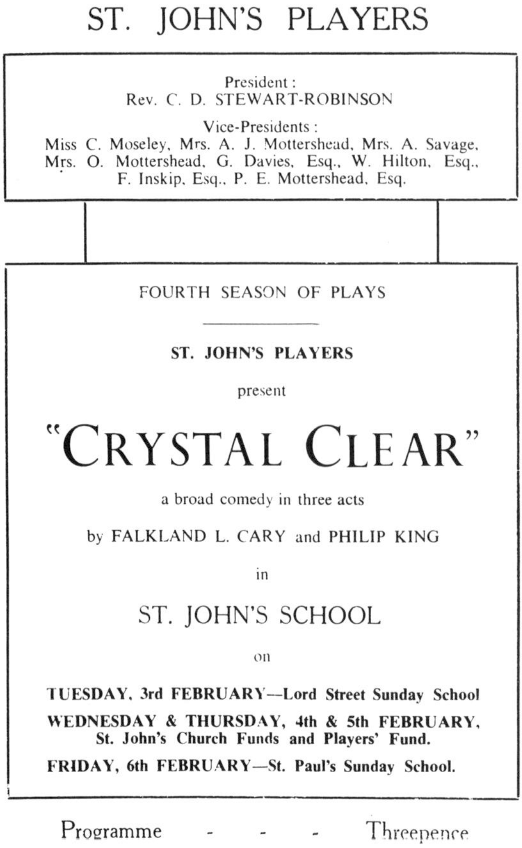

ST. JOHN'S PLAYERS

President :
Rev. C. D. STEWART-ROBINSON

Vice-Presidents :
Miss C. Moseley, Mrs. A. J. Mottershead, Mrs. A. Savage,
Mrs. O. Mottershead, G. Davies, Esq., W. Hilton, Esq.,
F. Inskip, Esq., P. E. Mottershead, Esq.

FOURTH SEASON OF PLAYS

ST. JOHN'S PLAYERS

present

"CRYSTAL CLEAR"

a broad comedy in three acts

by FALKLAND L. CARY and PHILIP KING

in

ST. JOHN'S SCHOOL

on

TUESDAY, 3rd FEBRUARY—Lord Street Sunday School
WEDNESDAY & THURSDAY, 4th & 5th FEBRUARY,
St. John's Church Funds and Players' Fund.
FRIDAY, 6th FEBRUARY—St. Paul's Sunday School.

Programme   -   -   -   Threepence

Programme for a post-war production by St John's players.

to become the famed operatic bass Forbes Robinson. St Michael's and St John's churches both had their own dramatic societies. The Hovis society presented their plays in the Morton Hall (one, I remember, being that old favourite When we are Married) and BWA had its own team of actors and actresses.

Villages like Henbury and Over Alderley also mustered their dramatic societies. However, the most important development as it turned out was the inauguration of the Macclesfield Amateur Dramatic Society, formed with the help of some members of the Central School society which had grown overlarge with the return of the soldiers.

The original society, now more snappily called the Central School Players, continued with productions by John Fytton, playing first in the Parochial Hall in Roe Street (where I made my acquaintance with Rebecca) and then the Brocklehurst Memorial Hall.

I remember these things because I had by now become a junior reporter on the *Macclesfield Times*, and consequently acted as a stand-in drama critic. After all, I had some genuine dramatic experience, for had I not taken part in Henbury Youth Fellowship's entry in the Macclesfield Youth Festival drama section? In a borrowed dog collar I played the curate – shades of things to come – in a one-act excerpt from Outward Bound. Modesty forbids me to give you the result.

Poppy Poopah disclosed! Scene from the Central School Players' production of Rookery Nook.
Frank Snelson is on the left.

Two youngest members of the Central School Players present flowers to the two most senior at the
society's 21st celebration in 1950. Marjorie Brough, then working in the Times office, makes her
presentation to Florence Hanson. Alan Sefton is handing a buttonhole to John Fytton (out of picture).

Now when, with this slender experience, I began criticising the acting of others most of the societies, especially the smaller ones, greeted my resulting reviews if not with enthusiasm then at least with dignified silence. However, that was not the case with the Central School Players. I can't remember what part of my comments on Rebecca nettled them, but I was made aware that one of the society's leaders had represented to the editor that I was too young to criticise their efforts, and thereafter I was banished to plays staged in the outer villages.

However, John Fytton must have forgiven me for I was so far inspired as to audition for a small part in one of the Central School Players productions, and got it. When I made this known in the office, however, the new editor, the redoubtable A J Wood (whom we have already met in more embarrassing circumstances) indicated that he preferred me to spend my time in the evenings at shorthand classes. So I did.

Thereafter the curtain came down on my theatrical career, and I left the town for 20 years, during which the number of amateur dramatic societies declined. But I have the happiest memories of those days when friendships were brightened by the footlights, and hearts were lightened by laughter, and one medium-sized town could boast any number of Merle Oberons, Ralph Richardsons and Robertson Hares.

16

Four Wheels Good, Two Wheels Better!

My love affair with motorbikes began in the war, and like all affairs became more intense because the object of affection proved elusive. No new bikes were available in those years – they all went to the forces. Second-hand ones were scarce, I had no adult relatives with motorcycling inclinations, and I was in any case far too young to go out on the road.

But I admired them from afar. Our household began to take Motorcycling magazine – the green one, distinct from The Motor Cycle which had a blue cover and to us seemed inferior. Within its pages were nostalgic articles about bikes of the past, announcements from manufacturers about the bikes they would produce after the war, and three or four columns of small ads for old bikes. It was here that I first heard of the dozens upon dozens of names of British-built bikes, almost all of which have now vanished – BSA, Douglas, Scott, Rudge. Just looking at the ads now brings tears to the eyes – a 350cc Velocette for £14, a 250cc Enfield for £30, a 1926 Ariel 500 for a measly £6.10s! No wonder schoolboys dreamed in those days.

Jack Parker: one of the favourites

But mostly it had to remain a dream. From my reading I selected a 250cc Ariel as the first motorbike I would have of my own (it wasn't) and in the meantime we made do with whatever was to hand. My very first motorbike ride came through the courtesy of the brothers Joe and Harry Barlow. About a dozen lads were playing one evening in the old recreation ground off Pexhill Road when the Barlows rode over the field from their home on their bike, and gave all of us a ride in turn, sitting on the petrol tank. More activity was provided unknowingly by Keith Willies's father, working then at Woodford, who had a little New Imperial he was doing up in his spare time. When he wasn't at home we took turns in being pushed up and down the drive. But it was very tame without an engine.

We came close to disaster through the visit to our home of a cousin who was a captain, no less, in the Royal Artillery, and as such had the

The famous Tommy Simister, TT rider and garage owner

use of a 350cc Army bike. He parked it in the drive, and in our efforts to get astride and twist its throttle we tipped it over, to his great displeasure.

Once in the woods at Henbury we found a complete if slightly rusted belt-driven bike simply dumped there. For some unaccountable reason we left it where it was, which we wouldn't do now. Then on a visit to my favourite scrapyard in Swettenham Street I acquired for half a crown a complete motorbike engine which I tied to my bike and pushed home (I see now that this was the wrong way round – it should have pushed me).

At least we got near to actual working machines, and certainly within ear-splitting distance of them, at the speedway, to which for a time we became addicted. It was our good fortune that the only operating speedway track in Britain during the war was at Belle Vue, a relaxing, meandering train journey away along the old Bollington and Marple line. We aimed to arrive there in the middle of the afternoon, enjoy some rides in the fair, attempt to drink a mug of their terrible unsweetened tea, and then crowd into the stadium. A great thrill this was, especially if you stood on the corner so that the revving machines sent a shower of cinders cascading over you.

Here we quickly established our favourite riders like Jack and Norman Parker, Eric Chitty and Bill Kitchen. Whatever club they rode for before the war, they all appeared at Belle Vue during it. Riders in each race must of course have some distinguishing mark – you could hardly recognise them otherwise under their coat of cinders. So in each four-bike heat the riders would be identified by the blue, red, white or yellow cover on their helmet. This became important when, engine-less but still enthusiastic, we ran our own speedway races with pedal bikes on a lane leading to Highbirch farm at Pexhill. Here all was officially arranged, with a programme of four-rider heats scoring three points for a win, two for second and one for a third. The timekeeper at the finishing line round the bend could just see the starter's arm over the hedge, and when it fell he started counting. Soon afterwards a puffing, pedalling band of riders, each sporting a handkerchief or other bit of cloth of the right colour, would come dustily down the track and take a codged-up chequered flag. It was great fun while our strength lasted.

After I had left school I temporarily deserted my great love in favour of a green Evelyn Hamilton racing bike. I can't think why, since it was so energetic. We were out in the lanes one night, seeing how fast we could go, when we caught up with the rider of a two-stroke motorbike. Anxious to know how fast we were going we croaked at him: 'Speed?' But he thought we wanted to go faster, and disappeared into the distance in a haze of smoke.

While all this was going on my brother Philip had joined the ranks of motorcyclists, beginning with an old 250cc Francis Barnett two-stroke which was bought out of our father's demob allowance. He then progressed via a 250 BSA to a 350 girder-fork Panther. On this the two of us rode off with hundreds of others to Sunday's sporting events – hill climbs at Edale, scrambles at Pott Shrigley, grass track races at Hazel Grove. Philip was himself an intrepid rider. Once for a bet he attempted to ride UP the cobbles of Churchwallgate in top gear. This required a start way down in the Waters to get up speed, and it is true that he rocketed round the bend cheered on by a crowd of printers from the *Times* works. However, the bike's chugging got slower and slower until it expired almost exactly on the brow of the hill by the Parish Church. I call that a draw.

Sadly, Philip later had a collision with a lorry in Chester Road, causing serious injury to an arm and ending his motorcycling days.

In due course my pushbike craze exhausted both itself and me and in 1949, one year after I could legally have ridden a motorbike on the road, I acquired a new, sparkling, cream-and-chrome-tanked Panther 350cc. If I remind you that my grandfather was a Yorkshireman, and that Panthers were built at Cleckheaton in Yorkshire, you will understand the source of my good fortune. He always was a patriotic man.

The bike was bought from Arthur Watling, who had been an apprentice mechanic with the substantial local car and motor-cycle firm of Tommy Simister, himself a former TT rider. Arthur set up his own business after the war in what at first appeared to be a small shop in Buxton Road. Penetrating the mysteries of the shop, however, revealed what seemed to be a series of

Town's hero – Syd Gleave on one of his own SGS bikes ready for the 1929 TT.

underground passages, leading at one end to Arthur's office, and at the back
to a yard jam-packed with old bikes because there was nowhere else to put
them. Soon Arthur acquired an additional shop in Commercial Road, and later
still the Buxton Road premises were converted to provide a large showroom.
He also had a shop in Eagle Parade, Buxton

Most of my early encounters with Arthur took place in his subterranean
office. As my enthusiasm grew and came to embrace a dream of racing fame,
I had many such encounters concerning the purchase or exchange of a
succession of bikes, and I came to admire Arthur's impeccable technique and
cherubic smile as he gently persuaded customers that the bike they wanted for
£75 was really still a bargain at £95. I always left convinced he had done me
a great favour.

It's probably a libel, but Arthur and his merry men had a reputation for use
of the big hammer to solve intractable mechanical problems on the bikes they

Cyril Taylor, former mayor and vintage motor bike enthusiast, with the SGS he restored..

were repairing. But the bikes of those days were not so refined as the marvels of today. You would as soon take a hammer to a modern Honda as attempt to repair a Rolex with a wrench, but the old BSAs and Enfields and so on seemed to thrive on rough treatment.

There was quite a gang of enthusiasts who bumped into each other (figuratively speaking) at Arthur's, and you came to know them as much by their bikes as by their names. There was Arthur (BSA 350) Charlesworth, and a dental technician (Douglas 350) Scragg, and my friend Ron (BSA 250) Spratt. Most of us were in the Macclesfield Motorcycle Club, with stalwarts like Sid Shackley – who had *his* own shop in Sunderland Street – and Syd Blackshaw and Jessie. We went off for runs on Sundays, and soon I was joining in club trials in the hills around Wildboarclough and Tegg's Nose. This led me to think of trying my hand at grass track racing.

I had before me the example of the town's motorcycling hero, Syd Gleave, who not only built around 60 of his own Syd Gleave Special or SGS machines at his garage in Davenport Street, but also raced his own and other bikes in everything from grass tracks and speed trials to the TT. In 1933, as all the town knows, he won the Lightweight TT on an Excelsior, and on his own SGS bike in 1930 he came fourth. In the war he went on to become a test pilot.

Though I never met him personally I do remember meeting one of his SGS bikes as I passed by the garage one day in the war. And I was one of the gang of boys who on September 11, 1944, gazed silently at the wreckage of his Lancaster bomber which had crashed on test only an hour or two before, killing both Syd and his flight engineer. Altogether I was so impressed by Syd's story that in 1981 I produced a 60-page book about him. One of its readers, Sydney Bull, of Robin Lane, Chelford, wrote to me later to pay a moving tribute to Syd's sportsmanship. His lasting memory of Syd, he said, was of a grass track held at the Moss Rose soccer ground. The two of them met in the final where Syd, astride his racing SGS, and already an established racing rider, could have romped away from his opponent's 172cc Francis Barnett. But, being the sportsman he was, he won by just a few yards to save Mr Bull's face.

Traces of Syd's original garage can still be made out in the premises now used in Davenport Street as a Kwik-fit tyre and exhaust depot. My researches lead me to believe that there are only two surviving SGS bikes today. One, a two-stroke, was kept by Syd's nephew Philip in one of the premises used by Gleave Motors before it closed. The other, possibly a TT bike, was found as a wreck in a barn at Adlington and has now been restored by Cyril Taylor of Plumley.

Well, with all this history you will be wondering when I am going to tell you about my own racing career. The answer is, there isn't much to tell. Owing to my constant attendance at Arthur's premises (when I should have been at the *Times*) he allowed me from time to time to act as a temporary unpaid member of his staff and help out by towing in bikes that had broken down, tracking down second-hand bikes for sale, and that sort of thing. As a reward for my services he sold me for £35 a 350cc Velocette which I took to grass track races at Newcastle and Chester, with total lack of distinction. I then swapped the Panther for a 500cc BSA (the most beloved of my bikes) and with

TO-DAY'S RIDERS

SOLO

No.	Name	Town	C.C.	Machine
3	A. R. ELLISON, Birmingham		350 Triumph & 500 A.R.E Spec.	
4	R. TIMMS, Birmingham	...	...	350 A.R.E. Special
5	C. H. HAYDOCK, Woodhouse	...	...	500 Royal Enfield
6	C. A. ALLEN, Leicester	...	...	350 Triumph
7	D. WILLIAMS, Loughborough	...	...	497 Ariel
8	R. CRAMP, Shepshed	...	...	497 Ariel
11	V. J. NEEDHAM, Queniborough	...	...	348 Ariel
16	J. F. RILEY, Chilwell	...	...	350 Ariel J.A.P.
17	J. W. WELLER, Loughborough	...	...	490 Norton E.S.2
18	R. BROCKLEHURST, Mansfield	...	...	348 Burdett Special
20	W. LANCASTER, Macclesfield	...	...	350 & 500 Specials
24	P. BANKS, Coventry	...	...	349 B.S.A.

Among the riders at Loughborough grass track races in 1950 – Macclesfield's Bill Lancaster

this raced at Nantwich and Pickmere. The latter was the most spectacular of all the circuits since the riders, in close formation from the start, had to swoop down a steep hill towards the lake, then brake and turn sharply to the left before tackling a steep hill up and back to the start again. It was great fun, but again at these races I failed to trouble the scorer, as they say in cricket.

However, Macclesfield had worthier representatives than I at this sport. Russ Oldfield was the up and coming star, who went on to ride in the TT. Another Macclesfield stalwart was Bill Lancaster, still a regular attender at autojumbles buying his bits and pieces. He rode in many grass track races, both in Cheshire and Staffordshire.

Though motorcyclists think it can never happen, the time came when for convenience or for dryness four-wheeled transport seemed to have advantages over two. I had kept an eye on the car world. I had discovered that, as was the case with bikes, the ills of motors could be cured by fairly drastic treatment. I was present at many operations at Hardy's forge, in a yard down by the British Legion in Chestergate, where things were done to old Austins and Morrises which modern models simply couldn't stand. Mr Hardy, as adept at shoeing horses as mending cars, used to perk up motor springs by dipping them red-hot into a tub of oil, and he could wield a nifty hammer, too, when axles or track rods were bent.

I also enjoyed the work of the Perry brothers, who lived in Whirley Road and once built me a dainty body on the remains of an old Austin Seven Swallow. Later on they bought it back, cut through the propeller shaft, fitted

a second gearbox and, when last seen, were using the thing as a tractor. I was lost in admiration.

However, I have to say that cars simply didn't have the sporting image I liked to savour. We did go once or twice to see car trials in the hills round Buxton. There competitors like Dorothy Corbishley, whose family had a garage at the bottom of Jordangate exactly where the monster junction of the new road with Hibel Road now stands, tried to bounce their way up steep and greasy slopes. And I kept a proper boyish eye on the new crop of cars that were produced after the war. I noted, for example, the appearance on the roads of Macclesfield of the first Jowett Javelin, driven by a Mr Walker of Broken Cross — the name of that fortunate gentleman stays in my mind, you see. The Javelin appealed to me as a beautifully styled car, but it went the way of other British creations.

Not so beautiful was the slab-sided Singer 1500 saloon, an example of which appeared in Ford and Challinor's showroom next to the Picturedrome in 1946. I went in hoping to put my grandfather's name down on the waiting list — although he didn't know it — but the salesman advised me that the queue was already too long. Well, I didn't really like the car, anyway.

Now the years have slowed down, and my transport is a sedate Peugeot car, and it does all that I ask of it which isn't too much. But one day, I know, the old flame will burn again, and I shall long to get out on two wheels and smell the petrol leaking from the carburettor and mop up the oil spilled on the drive. What joyful times those were. I must say I take it as a personal affront that so many makes of motorbike simply vanished from the British scene. All those names I learned in boyhood, all those models I coveted, all (or almost all) have gone. In tribute to them, and to keep alive their memory, I offer this verse:

Beeza And Friends

AJS and Matchless, Douglas, James and Bown,
Built to rouse the countryside and deafen half a town.
Panthers gave a roar and the Corgis had a bark –
Thought they'd run for ever but
        they seemed to lose their spark.

HRD with Vincent, Raleigh, Rex and Rudge –
Mornings in the winter when the kickstart wouldn't budge.
Twistgrip on the handlebars, lever for the choke –
Thought they'd last for ever but
        they've all gone up in smoke.

Beeza had a Bantam and the Ariel had a Colt,
Arthur's lads could mend 'em with a hammer, nut and bolt.
OHV meant speed while the side valves pulled a load –
Thought they'd go for ever but
        they all ran out of road.

Sunbeam, Sun and Diamond, Excelsior and Dot,
Footchange came from Velo, the crackle came from Scott.
OK reigned Supreme, and Superior was the Brough.
Should have run for ever but
        the going got too tough.

Eagles flew from Coventry, and Indians from the North.
SG built a Special (and in one TT came fourth).
Two and four-stroke motors, Villiers and JAP –
Thought they'd sell for ever but
        they ended up as scrap.

Francis Barnett, Norman, Ambassador and Greeves ...
With ABC we started and with Zenith take our leaves.
All of these we've mentioned, and a hundred other makes –
We thought they'd go for ever but
        the world put on the brakes.

17

Stomping At The Stanley, Singing in The Choir ...

One of our eminent astronomers, when he comes down to earth and relaxes in his living room, is sitting on the very spot where scores of earnest young people once learned to waltz and quickstep and perhaps even tango.

This curious state of affairs comes about because he lives in what used to be Henbury School, scene of our parties and whist drives and – as we grew up and began our contacts with the fair sex – our dances.

They began, naturally enough, in a very haphazard sort of way, as part of what used to be called socials. These provided a bit of entertainment, a bit of whist or beetling, and just a bit of dancing, which the lads tried to pick up as they went along but about which the girls were a little more serious. Music for these hops was provided sometimes by records on a wind-up gramophone, sometimes by Mr Hough on his fiddle, and just occasionally by me, sweating and grimly determined at the piano while a serious dancer kept trying to tell me the rhythm I should be playing.

When I could join the others on the floor I soon learned the basic form of waltz and quickstep, provided my partner also learned to keep out of the way of my flying toes. This was followed by the occasional decorous barn dance, or a frantic Blaze Away with the two-step. Our efforts caused much amusement to the adults sitting round the walls – after all, we were part of the entertainment – though they did get a bit alarmed when we turned to the palais glide where you go down on one knee, up with the other and stamp stamp stamp. Thus: Poor little AngeLINE STAMP STAMP. I cannot believe now that there was room for a line of six or eight of us, arm in arm, to do this violent dance without the risk of serious damage to spectators or the building, and it amazes me that the astronomer found a livingroom left to sit in.

After two or three years of this apprenticeship, dancing to the war tunes of the time like New American Patrol and Victory Moon, we considered ourselves ready

Macclesfield Young Liberals

A

DANCE

with KEN PARR'S
MODERNAIRES BAND at the

Brocklehurst Memorial Hall

Friday, January 10th,
1947.

Novelty Items.
                    Attractive Prizes.

Tickets 3/6.   :   Buffet.

Take your partners at the old Stanley Hall for a Hockey Club dance in 1947. Music was supplied by the Astorians band.

to spread our wings, especially as we were now experiencing the joys of ever-so-proper contact with young ladies. 'Hold hands with the left, the right hand *lightly* on her back, and not too close together'. But even this was a delight.

We launched ourselves into this larger world, as far as I remember, at the dancing school of Doug and Ray Bailey, over the shops at the far end of Chestergate. We arrived there, rushing up the stairs, in the obligatory large and giggling group, and our cup of joy ran over literally because Super Snacks was only a few doors away and there between sessions on the dance floor we could chat to new acquaintants. This was a new world. Up to then we had danced only with girls we had known (it seemed) all our lives. The new freedom was made possible largely by the ever-popular Paul Jones dance which supplied you with a steady stream of new partners chosen by fate when the music stopped. This gave us the chance to polish up our skills in social chat. 'Do you come here often?' 'Only during the mating season'. Ah, how witty it all sounded.

From Doug Bailey's we graduated to the larger public dance halls in the town, like the Parochial Hall in Roe Street which began life as a noncomfor-

A 1949 dance in the Parochial Hall, organised by Macclesfield Music Festival. Alderman Breese is seated centre.

mist chapel, became a parish meeting place for St Alban's, and is now the Salvation Army citadel. In our day plays and concerts were put on downstairs, dances took place upstairs. Here, for the first time as a regular feature, we danced to one or other of the local bands. There were some with extraordinary names – the Rhythmagicians Swingtet, for example. On a more prosaic note we encountered also the Blue Jays, Ken Parr and his Modernaires, the Astorian Swingtet, and Jack Gill's Embassy Band.

Very soon those of us who were self-taught, and liked it that way, became acquainted with an unpalatable fact. Some of our friends were actually taking professional lessons in dancing, and studying for medals, from bronze upwards. Extraordinary! Jean Rowbotham, Rhoda Dawson, the Nouvelle dancing studio – these and other experts attempted to bring a little discipline and professionalism to the local hop. But what did we care? One or two managed by themselves to learn such delicate footwork as the quickstep feather, which took you and your partner twinkling down the middle of the floor like Rogers and Astaire. For the rest, getting as close to the partner as decorum permitted continued to be of more importance than the synchronisation of steps, and we barged along as before.

Now and then we had a change of venue and took to the floor at King's School for the traditional old boys' dances. It was there that Sheila and I met, finding ourselves sitting side by side on a bench in the dining hall during a break from dancing. I remember she had a red dress and we each had an orange juice. What mighty works from chance encounters grow! Soon we were regular partners on the dance-floor of life, and have waltzed along merrily ever since. So there is another thing for which I must thank King's School.

Of all the dances in the town, however, I suppose our most regular rendez-vous was at the Stanley Hall on a Saturday night. The Stanley Hall deserves remembrance. You got into it between two huge stone pillars in the gently-curving row of shops and offices leading down from the Post Office in Castle Street. The imposing entrance led into a wide corridor off which were the offices of the Macclesfield Conservative Association. All this is now part of the Grosvenor Centre, so it is more or less where the indoor market now stands that we in our day hoofed it round the floor with 200 or 300 of our friends and acquaintances, happy and carefree.

At these dances the regular drummer was Sheila's cousin Sam Davenport, and through his intervention I was allowed to sing with the band. 'How can you buy Killarney' was my first rendition, But I was willing to try my voice at anything even when, as it turned out, I didn't know the words. I remember singing also when the same band played at Lower Withington village hall.

One of the more rumbustious dances at this time, in which everyone loved to join, was the Hokey-Cokey. You know, the one that begins with you putting your left arm in, and ends with everyone rushing into the middle in a glorious mix-up. I enjoyed this as much as the rest until, much later, I heard an odd and rather unpleasant suggestion of its true origin. The title phrase, it may be, goes back through several amendments to the time of the Reformation, and incor-porates a Protestant jibe at the actions of a Catholic priest. Hokey Cokey, in this explanation, is a corruption of the words of consecration at the Mass, Hoc est enim corpus meum, or This is my body. And some of the words we sang – 'Knees bend, arms stretch', make the connection even plainer. Since hearing this I have never fancied doing the Hokey-Cokey, even if I had the energy.

On really grand occasions we wound up at the Town Hall. This was the venue of the annual Press Balls held after the war. For these Cliff Rathbone and the other senior journalists used to twist a few arms and perhaps call in a few favours to ensure the presence of the mighty men of the town – the Mayor and councillors and police chief and so on. It was largely a black tie occasion for the men, evening dresses for the ladies, and all profits went to Press charities.

This was a time of strange speciality dances, as well as the Hokey Cokey, and another one I remember was Balling the Jack made popular for some reason by Danny Kaye. 'First you put your two knees close up tight', we warbled, suiting the actions to the words. It sounds most questionable now, but it must have been all right because we danced it at the Press Ball which was the epitome of respectability.

As well as being the scene of these splendid triumphs, the Town Hall was for me the site of a fearful disaster. By the end of the forties with, as I have said, youth culture beginning to push to the fore, it was thought desirable to give young people a bit of responsibility and dignity, heaven help us. This thinking led to the formation of the Macclesfield Youth Council, composed of representatives from church fellowships and other clubs. It elected its own mayor, R Wright, and town clerk, John Dobson, discussed matters affecting young people, and then in 1949 got ambitious and organised a youth ball at the Town Hall. We aimed high, and booked a 'broadcasting band' from Stockport. Alas, despite some of us standing on the pavement outside and desperately begging passers-by to come in, the event flopped and lost £30. This was beyond our individual means, but the band and others demanded payment, so what could we do?

By this time I had become Youth Mayor, and inherited the odium of the whole fiasco. There was a frigid meeting with Mr Ashness, the education officer, under whose department the youth council operated. I squirmed considerably before it was agreed that the band and other creditors should be paid out of local authority funds. But I never want to organise another youth ball, and it was a relief when advancing years took away the possibility that I should ever have to do so again.

But that was an exception. For the most part our dances were a delight, their tickets a passport to excitement and romance. There were different halls and different bands and sometimes even different girls. But some things never changed. There were the MCs in their smart suits announcing the dances; the anticipation (or sometimes dread) of the ladies' excuse-me, the suspense of spot prizes, and finally the smoochy melancholy of the last waltz. It's time to say goodnight, and Who's taking you home tonight ... I'll be loving you, always.

Singing in The Choir

Macclesfield has a great musical tradition. Probably, as in so many other towns and especially in Wales, this stems from the halcyon days when there was a church in every big street, and a choir in every church. These were first-class training grounds, and there were regular chances for the singers to show their talents at choir festivals and choir sermons and in such popular works as Maunder's Olivet to Calvary.

In addition to that, in the harder days gone by, making music helped to provide some release from the grinding toil of the day and the spectre of poverty. There can be no doubt that music does send the soul soaring – I remember once visiting the now vanished Mount Tabor chapel off Windmill Street and hearing a choir singing 'God so loved the world' from Stainer's Crucifixion, and believing that I had never heard anything so beautiful.

There is no doubt either that an element of competition can add a spur to singing. At a Christ Church festival before the war I heard young lads striving to outdo the famous Ernest Lush as they warbled 'O for the wings of a dove'. On a larger scale there was the annual Macclesfield Music Festival which, before and just after the war, used to fill room after room at the Large Sunday School (now the Heritage Centre) with the sound of music. It continues now in Ryles Park school.

One year my brother Philip was among the competitors at the Large Sunday School as a violinist in a quintet entered by his music teacher, Mr Mitchell of 50 Prestbury Road. He also took over as my piano teacher and was a rather stern figure, as he needed to be. We two boys went for lessons together and one week, setting off to walk from Henbury as was our custom, we fell to arguing about which was the shortest route to Prestbury Road – via Chester Road or Victoria Road. We decided to put the matter to the test, Philip taking the former route and I the latter. Philip had his violin but I, not having my piano with me, carried the music. I arrived at Mr Mitchell's house to find him with a face like thunder, and Philip looking pleased with himself. They had waited ten minutes for me to turn up and had been unable to start Philip's lesson because of course there was no music.

Mr Mitchell was also, inadvertently, the cause of the only physical punishment I remember as a boy. I was due at my piano lesson that week on Saturday morning but, passing the sandpit in Chelford Road, I saw an army of men with attendant and eager little boys filling sandbags for the protection of the town. It occurred to me – and I believe it still – that labouring in defence of one's country was a more patriotic endeavour than a mouldy piano lesson, and I pitched in with a shovel. My grandfather, who had to pay for the lesson whether I turned up or not, did not see the matter in so clear a light when I reported the matter to him, and for once chastised me. I was duly mortified.

Well, having faced the music, let's return to it. The annual youth festival, organised after the war, gave the town's young people their own chance to show their talents. There were competitions in all sorts of activities, from the writing of poetry to singing and the playing of instruments, as well as drama. Secretary of the whole enterprise was Mr Allen, who used to work in Holland and Barwoods and whom I was pestering for results for the papers when he should have been serving customers. In this festival Henbury youth fellowship won the choir competition for two years in succession, conducted by the redoubtable Dick Hankinson and singing 'Linden Lea' and 'All in the April evening'

KAᵢTHLEEN FERRIER
Contralto.

★

PARK STREET METHODIST CHURCH

CHOIR FESTIVAL

Sunday, April 15th, 1945.

★

ELIZABETH BOENDERS Violin
HARRY G. WHITTER   Organ
JAMES MAYCOCK, Conductor

Chairmen:
2-30: J. F. MORTON, Esq. 6-30: Ald. T. M. ABRAHAM, J.P.

Prayers by Rev. P. S. Johnson, B.A.

AUGMENTED CHOIR

Combined Programme   2/6

Programme, signed by Kathleen Ferrier, for a memorable choir festival.

In all these musical endeavours the town was well served by Mr Jones and his music store, which fortuitously was placed next door to the *Times* office in Queen Victoria Street. Thus I was able to dash in and out to buy the latest song hit or take advice from Mr Jones and his assistant Winifred Bamford on suitable music for piano studies. Once, having heard it on the radio, I went in to order Chopin's Fantaisie Impromptu, the one with 'I'm always chasing rainbows' in the middle. When the music came Mr Jones glanced at it as he handed it over, shook his head and said: 'You'll never play that'. How right he was.

One Christmas the *Times* decided to give the staff a party – at the Macclesfield Arms, no less – and offers of entertainment were called for. With Jean Kimpton, who worked in the office, I thought it would be a good idea to introduce a note of culture and provide a couple of piano duets. But where to rehearse? In Mr Jones's music store at lunch time, of course, so in full view and earshot of passers-by we practised long and hard and eventually entranced our party audience with Teddy Bears' Picnic and the Volga Boat Song, by way of encore whether they wanted it or not.

But all this was small beer compared to the major musical offerings which delighted the town. Some of the ambitious church and chapel choirs brought in professional soloists to boost their festivals, and I remember going to one at the old Park Street chapel before the war. I recall the blazing lights shining on an audience which seemed to reach to the ceiling, and a wonderful hush of reverence and attention. After the war this tradition continued for some years, with festivals in the chapels and the same choirs with star soloists presenting concert versions of Merrie England and Tom Jones in venues such as Lord Street.

My Auntie Alice, who sang with the Park Street choir, told me often about the great kindness of these visiting singers. It was a matter of pride if the ladies of the choir could announce that they had stood just behind or within touching distance of this great singer or that, for they could shine then with a reflected glory. Mary Jarred was a great favourite, and she and the other notables cheerfully gave their autographs to the choir members.

Perhaps the most memorable of these choir festivals was one on April 15, 1945, when the star visitor was Kathleen Ferrier, then just launching out on her glittering career. At two services she sang 15 songs, some of them with the choir, and they included 'I will lay me down in peace', which she had just recorded, and 'Art thou troubled?', which came to be a great favourite with her audiences.

I wasn't at the festival but – and this is the point I am trying to make about the way memory can strengthen and comfort – I know just how it must have looked and sounded. I had seen the chapel packed and attentive; I have since

The smiles of success – J L Riley and his choir after they had won the Festival of Britain competition in 1951.

heard that glorious voice singing these very songs. I can hear the notes now, thrilling the audience squeezed in pews and gallery, the song pouring out while all the rest was silence:

'Art thou weary? Rest shall be thine'.

Glorious stuff indeed. What pleasure and inspiration such music brings.

But perhaps the greatest musical achievement for Macclesfield in these years was the victory by the J L Riley Festival Choir in the 1951 Festival of Britain competitions, held at the Royal Festival Hall in June. The choir, formed by John Riley in 1929 and achieving great success, had qualified for the finals of both the ladies' and mixed choirs through victory in regional qualifying contests.

For the great event they travelled to London on June 21, staying for four days. The ladies, wearing new hyacinth blue dresses in Macclesfield silk, the material for which had been given by BWA, sang in their final on June 22, and came third behind choirs from Southend and Plymouth.

The 60 members of the mixed choir had their big day on June 23 and they were drawn to sing tenth out of the 14 choirs in the final. Mr Riley confessed later to apprehension about the fine performance of the Huddersfield choir. In the final adjudication it was Huddersfield who were leading from the halfway mark with 186 points. They were still ahead when for some reason only the marks of the Riley choir had still to be announced. The reason for this suspense was revealed when the judge came at last to their score – 189. They had won, and furthermore it was Princess Elizabeth who presented the Glasgow Orpheus trophy to Mr Riley.

Our old friend Harry Hayes, showing fine journalistic judgment, had travelled to London and was therefore on the spot to record the triumph. The *Macclesfield Times* made up for lost ground by printing on art paper a special edition of that week's Times, splashing with the story of the Festival Hall victory, and presenting a copy to every member of the choir. A civic reception was arranged for the choir, and this was held before a packed audience at the choir's home base, Wesley's Chapel in Sunderland Street, a fortnight later. Congratulations to Mr Riley and the choir were led by the mayor, Mrs A M White.

Later the choir, as a mark of their respect, decided to donate the trophy to Mr Riley as his personal possession 'knowing he would treasure it more than rubies or gold'.

So ended probably the finest hour in the history of Macclesfield's music, a history that embraces, as we have seen, music to dance to, and to sing, and to use in worship. As Mr Riley said, in tune with the Bard: 'If music be the food of love, play on'. There is no doubt that Macclesfield will.

18

Caution – Men And Women at Work

There are few things in life more satisfying than watching other people work. Like Jerome K Jerome, I like work so much that I could sit and look at it for hours – provided someone else is doing it. Now that is just what a boy has every opportunity of doing, and I took full advantage of the fact. People, I find, are not averse to explaining to an interested bystander just what it is they are up to.

I can't pretend this is what happened with the first 'man at work' I remember watching – he was at the time standing ten feet above me on the driving platform of his steamroller, and I was about three. His interesting, smoking and clanking machine was parked in Langford Street at the time, in between journeys to and fro in Chester Road which was being resurfaced. I stood at the corner to watch, and young as I was I marvelled at the vigorous turns of a wheel and yanks on a lever that were needed to change the direction of the steamroller from forward to back and back again. I know now that the driver worked so furiously so as to make the time spent at rest between each direction – what is known technically as the 'dwell' – as short as possible, and the roller wouldn't sink into the hot tar. I'm sure the man would have told me that had I been able to frame the question. But isn't it interesting?

That is just the sort of fascinating titbit you pick up from watching people at work. Two more of my long-suffering tutors were the Cleaver brothers, who came from time to time to paint our house. The task started with the mixing of paint to achieve the shade desired by my grandmother, and I watched entranced as one Mr Cleaver would take instruction, then mix in a little more blue, only to be told it was now too blue. So he would try a bit of white, and then the blue was too pale. This went on, with more toing and froing, for some time, before my grandmother had to admit that 'perhaps that's a bit like the colour I want', and with that the Cleavers sprang into action to slap the paint on before she changed her mind again.

But best of all was the discovery that some old paint had to be burned off, and out came the blowlamp. This was exciting because there was always the chance that they would burn the house down, but they never did. Still, it was worth watching just in case.

Then there was Mr Shaw, the electrician. He lived in Whirley Road, but he might just as well have lived with us for the number of times he had to be called. This was during the period when I was making a practical study of

The place is unknown, but the sentiments are clear – a Macclesfield mill at a time of celebration.

electricity and its peculiar ways. I found it amazing that so many things could blow a fuse. Once, when my mother complained of the cold, I scoured the town and found in Woolworths a little circular element for an electric fire. In no time I had made a frame for it from a biscuit tin, but I put the terminals on the back too close to the metal and, in a phrase made famous by Flanders and Swan, 'out went all the lights'. It was no wonder that my electrical activities were sternly discouraged, but at least I can say it was watching Mr Shaw that made me what I am in the do-it-yourself world.

A cobbler at Broken Cross, Mr Sowerbutts, fascinated me with the number of tacks he could hold in his mouth and the neatness with which he could drive them into the leather. And the assistants at the Co-op grocery store at the Cross had another skill that any small boy would envy. As I have said, I wasn't too keen on the mundane task of food shopping, but it was worth calling at the Co-op to see tiny quantities of butter being slapped into greaseproof paper, and sugar weighed out into little blue bags. But it was when the items for your food parcel had at last been assembled that the real tour de force occurred. They tied the brown paper parcel with string which they then snapped with their fingers. Amazing! My friends and I tried often and often to do this trick, but invariably ended up achieving nothing but sore fingers.

It is always a pleasure to watch a man who loves his work, and that is why, when I was helping my mother in the *Times* office during desultory days off school, I enjoyed the visits of Mr Ponting. He had a furniture store in

BWA's main weaving shed, around 1945.

Commercial Road, and what he liked doing was writing long and sometimes witty adverts proclaiming his wares. These always ended: 'If you're wanting, come to Ponting'. Each word of these adverts had to be counted so his bill could be worked out, and I fancy that part of the fun for Mr Ponting was seeing my mother and me each having a go at counting this long, long list and each arriving at a different answer. We had to go on until we could both agree, then Mr Ponting paid up and departed, smiling.

Another attraction for boys was watching holes being dug in the road or – to bring the story up to date in Macclesfield – trenches in all the pavements. Then, if we had half an hour to spare, we could enjoy the spectacle of sacks being hauled up by chain from the pavement to the top of a mill, or down again. This took place most frequently at farmers' produce depots in Stanley Street, Samuel Street and Castle Street, and never failed to intrigue us, especially when the safety trap at the top snapped shut so nothing could fall down.

Talking of farmers brings me to the delight I found in the curious (to an outsider) activities known as ploughing matches and hedge-laying competitions. Though I was brought up on the fringe of the country I didn't come into contact with these pastimes until as a junior reporter I was commanded to attend them. I had to take a bus to some venue like Knutsford and then trudge through farm fields to reach the scene of the action. There I found dedicated men vying with each other to plough the straightest furrows with horse or tractor, or to cut and fold the neatest hedge.

These surely are among the most esoteric of displays. It cannot matter greatly to the crop if the furrow is arrow straight or bends a weeny bit. Yet here these experts met in day-long solemn rivalry, putting forth all their skill and strength for the sheer love of order and neatness, for the quiet pleasure of doing the very best they could. Remembrance of these occasions brings to mind an epitaph to a countryman by the poet Ernest Rhys, which ends:

'He could make a gate and dig a ditch and plough as straight as a stone can fall. And he is dead'.

That seems to restore a much-needed note of seriousness to the matter of people's labour. I began this chapter with some lighthearted references to men at work. But there was nothing lighthearted really about what I heard someone once describe in modern jargon as the 'learning of income generation skills' – in other words, the need to make a living. Meeting this need has in Macclesfield's famous silk industry involved hundreds of thousands of people over many generations in very hard labour indeed.

Working with silk has been going on in the town, in one way or another, from the seventeenth century, probably beginning with the making of silk buttons. At first people worked in cottages or small workshops, with only the power of their hands. But from the middle of the 18th century mills began to

EXPORT

HALLE'S Ltd.

EVENING CLASSES

The next term for Evening Classes will commence on THURSDAY, the 9th JANUARY, 1947, at 6-15 p.m.

Students will be welcomed for enrolment on Thursday, Friday and Saturday (until 12 noon), the 2nd, 3rd and 4th January, 1947.

HALLE'S Ltd.

PARK GREEN WORKS, MACCLESFIELD.

Evening classes for the workers.

make their appearance with machinery powered first by water, and then by steam. In the 50 years from 1800 the town's population soared from 8000 to almost 40,000. Many of the new houses built to accommodate the influx had garrets for the hand-loom weavers; but by the turn of the century most of the 10,000 people – a quarter of the population – who were estimated to be dependent on silk for their income were working for substantial manufacturers in mills.

There were spinners and weavers and throwsters, dyers and finishers, fringers and trimmers, printers by screen and block, hemmers and embroiderers. Masters then and later included the Brocklehursts and the Whistons (later to amalgamate into the mighty BWA complex), 'Gus' Hewetson and his embroidery empire, firms such as Windsmoor and Neckwear, and families like the Smales, Frosts, Heaths, Lomases, and Arnolds. Whole streets were dominated by the brick escarpments of mill walls, with their echelons of windows designed to let in the maximum amount of light. The view from Sparrow Park, behind the Parish Church, was a great arc from north to south of mill chimneys pouring out their smoke; the sound from a hundred doorways as you passed by was of clacking looms and whirring bobbins. At its busiest there were around a hundred major mills, and hundreds more minor enterprises located in rooms of houses or sheds

This was the scene I remember as an unaffected observer. But most people of my age have heard from older relatives and friends stories of the human

WINDSMOOR

(MACCLESFIELD) LTD.

GOOD

MACHINISTS

and

LEARNERS

Urgently Required

Clean, Light and Interesting Work.
Three Weeks Holiday with Pay.

Tea provided free morning and afternoon.
Excellent Canteen. **Five-Day Week.**

Apply MR. J. ARNOLD

New Victoria Mills, Waterside, Macclesfield.

Telephone 4407

---

effort and sometimes misery which were required to fuel this vast enterprise before, to everyone's disbelief, it all but vanished like a thief in the night.

My two aunts remembered with some awe the days when they were part-timers of 12 and 13, obliged to go to school for half the day, and allowed into the mills for the other half. At the appointed time for starting they had to dash through the streets in order to beat the hooter – a few seconds late and the gates were shut against them so that they missed the half-day's work and, more important, the half day's pay. As they grew up and became regular workers they faced being fined, or 'bated', if they were late.

The hours were long – 8am to 6pm on weekdays except in the couple of months leading up to the Christmas rush, when the workers were told (no choice allowed) to work until 8pm. Saturday hours were 8am to noon. The big rooms where the women worked, the weaving sheds or the spinning rooms, were each under the command of a 'missis', like Louie Hilton at Frost's. These forewomen are remembered sometimes as rather ferocious people, the female equivalent of a sergeant major, but it must have been difficult to keep reasonable order among four or five dozen women, each with their own personalities and some with their ambitions, and in any case the 'missis' would be watched by the next boss up the ladder, and he by another boss, and so on, so it was essential to show order and efficiency.

Still, the pick of the 'missises' are remembered with admiration and affection for doing their best for the workers under them. Many, like Nellie Redgate of Kershaws, who continued to be a regular worshipper at St George's into her nineties, were so respected by their charges that they maintained lifelong friendships with each other. And those who toiled in the big rooms recall a great sense of kinship, and a willingness to help any colleague in trouble.

Another of the stern but kindly characters was Bertha Flood, a missis at Arnolds. One day a mouse was detected in her room and a panic stampede began to get out. But Bertha stood alone, like Horatius at the bridge, and while 'those behind cried forward, and those before cried back', none was able to get past her.

From all this activity in the mills poured forth a steady stream of ties and belts, dress lengths and completed garments, scarves and 'fancies'. Coming up to the end of the war the big firms saw full order books ahead, and a need to keep up their workforce to meet the demand. BWA – annual profits around a third of a million pounds – listed for the benefit of young people leaving school in 1945 the jobs that had to be filled if the firm was to continue to flourish. Hoping to attract the 'brightest and best' school-leavers it went through the opportunities department by department. In the spinning mill, for example, headed by a manager, assistant manager, overlookers and charge-

Sewing for pleasure – St George's Ladies' Needlework Guild at work in 1947.

hands, there were 30 to 40 specialist jobs for which people were always needed, and these included such roles as bale breakers, draft pickers, uptwisters, multiple end cheese winders, and gassers.

Local papers at this time carried regular display adverts for staff, sometimes urgently required. Halle's in Park Green, among others, held evening classes, with formal term-times, for learners. There were rewards too for the loyal employees. In 1948 Hewetson's celebrated the 50th anniversary of the founding of the firm and could point with pride to an expanded empire that included the Albion mill in London Road, Regency Mill in Wardle Street and a new mill in Vincent Street, as well as premises from time to time in Kidsgrove, Oldham, Buxton, Urmston and Leek. At the celebration dinner the great Augustus William Hewetson announced that the firm was giving its 400 workers £1 for each year of service, adding up to a distribution of £5,000.

Now, bit by bit and sometimes brick by brick, these great silken empires have vanished. So have the solid family firms, like Arnold's with their memories of Uriah and James Arnold. Surprisingly, though, their ghosts can still come back and grab you unawares. If you take a turn around the town, along Catherine Street, maybe, or Green Street or Mill Road, a familiar clacking may come to your ears, and a dimly remembered smell of fabric to your nose, and you will know that indeed there are still silk firms at work in the home of silk. Or, to be more conveniently reminded of all that has gone before, you can still visit Cartwright and Sheldon's Paradise Mill which serves as a living museum.

In any case, some of the skills learned in this great industry, and some of the work put in, still survive in practical ways. Before and just after the war most churches and other organisations put sewing and other activities to good fund-raising purposes. My grandmother was a Vice President of Christ Church Ladies Guild, which met in a wooden hut across the road from the school and whose members, among other things, toiled throughout the year at various projects for the annual sales of work. The various efforts were directed by the 'work secretary'. Bedlinen and tablecloths were cut, hemmed and embroidered, gloves and scarves knitted, handkerchiefs packed and boxed, all to be produced at the big event. Supporters bought their thrift tickets through the year to be spent at the stalls, and many a bride bought her stock of household linens by this means.

Work like this still goes on, if not quite on the same scale. Fellowship learned at the weekly sewing sessions at St George's and St Paul's, the Parish Church and Wesley's, still brings the participants together in other friendly ways. The purpose of all this activity and busyness, all the toil and sometimes the heartbreak, I never did learn to question for very early on I had seen and memorised a poem that hung on the wall of one of my older relatives, and it seemed always so right for the town of Macclesfield:

Not till the loom is silent and the shuttle cease to fly,
Shall God unroll the canvas and explain the reason why
The dark threads are as needful in the weaver's skilful hands
As the threads of gold and silver in the pattern he has planned.

19

Holidays and Jolly Days

Barnaby has had a brief mention in an earlier chapter, but in a book about Macclesfield one mention hardly does the subject justice. It isn't generally known that if all the articles and leaflets written about the Barnaby holiday were stacked one on top of another they would form a pile higher than Blackpool Tower. But for old time's sake another millimetre or two won't matter.

So here's a quick dash through memories of Barnaby. Queues for the buses, queues for the trains, a few even waiting for their taxi. An army of little boys eager to carry your cases to the station, or push them there on an old pram for sixpence. The masses heading for Blackpool, the superior smiles of those venturing to the East Coast or even to Bournemouth. The determination of those who couldn't actually get a week off but who packed coaches for a day out, perhaps to New Brighton or Matlock or Trentham. Hearing talk of previous holidays and the places to avoid – like boarding houses that offered cake on the first night to give a good impression, and cake on the last night to leave a happy memory, but no cake in between. Other houses that charged sixpence 'for use of cruet'. Checking again the advert in the *Times* that had led you to book for a week with 'Mrs Bennett in Blackpool Central, homely board residence, 10s 6d daily', and wondering if it would be all right. OR, walking down Chestergate on the Saturday morning, usually bustling with shoppers, and finding just one friend to talk to because so many had fled to the seaside. Shops closed all over the place for a long weekend, or a week, sometimes even a fortnight. Hearing the groans and forebodings of those setting out for the Isle of Man – 'Terrible trip last time and he was sick all the way'. All the schools except King's and the High School closed down – but then there was no other break till Wakes in the autumn. Holidaymakers spending their pennies on wish-you-were-here cards for the folk back home – in just one week around 12,000 cards swamped the Macclesfield sorting office. Entertainments arranged for the stay-at-homes, especially in wartime, with band concerts in the parks.

And then ... the return. Buckets and spades looking forlorn as they were carried up Hibel Road. The handwritten menus set out on the table at home, trying to pretend we were still at the hotel. Eating the last of the rock and handing out gifts to friends, wishing we hadn't been so generous. The realisa-

Pack your trunk and do a
bunk to BLACKPOOL.

A clarion call to Blackpool at the height of its popularity between the wars.

tion, on the part of adults, that there must be another 50 weeks of work before Barnaby could come round again.

Yes, all too soon the great break came to an end. And all too soon came even more dramatic changes. A week in Blackpool stopped being the longed-for goal, the promised land of our dreams. Holidays in Spain changed to cruises in the Med, then to the Caribbean, perhaps round the world. And finally, not even any Barnaby to holiday in!

I do believe I was a witness to the beginning of this seachange in our holiday expectations. On a winter night around 1950 I was directed by the editor to go to Hibel Road station to see off the late train to London and interview some of the passengers going aboard. They were boys from King's, bound on the first school ski-ing trip to Austria, harbingers of a great army for whom a stick of rock, a pint of ale, and a show at the end of the pier would never again be enough.

However, back to the days when there were many simpler pleasures that kept up our peckers in between the formal holidays. Whenever possible, for example, there were fetes. Some I enjoyed as a boy, some I went to as a reporter. At the great Fanshawe Fete at Siddington I almost encountered that suave comedian Gillie Potter. I discovered, however, that as he was the star attraction he was appearing not with the common-or-garden crowds but in a separate enclosure behind a hedge with an extra charge to watch. So though I heard him 'speaking to us in English', I and the other skinflints didn't actually see him.

Another fete was held in the great field in front of the old Henbury Hall – almost on our doorstep, in fact. Here I found the farm lads competing to see who could pick up a bale of straw on a pitchfork and hurl it the highest. It was like a high jump, with the bar constantly being moved up. They made it look easy; it wasn't.

The opening of these events was then quite a formal affair, with speakers anxious to give the captive audience the full flavour of their oratorical powers. Sometimes the coughing and shuffling of the impatient crowd could be quite embarrassing as they wanted to get on with the various activities. It was therefore a pleasure at Henbury school to come across, for the first time, an opener who quoted the golden rule for these occasions. It was the father of my friend Derek Wood who said simply: 'I have been advised to stand up, speak up and shut up'. Having done all three he sat down again within 20 seconds, to rapturous applause. I have tried to apply this lesson to sermons.

Most of the fetes had special attractions on the scale, if not in the style, of Gillie Potter. Thus, you could bowl for a pig (but where would you keep it if you won?) or enter baby in a baby show. At a couple of postwar fetes at Bosley that I remember you could watch a demonstration of strength by the local

St George's Rose Queen, Irene Hulley, on her big day just before the second world war. The little attendants, dressed like the queen in the best that Macclesfield could provide, are Betty Ashley (right) and Sheila Latham.

tug-of-war team, then at the height of its powers. Some had fiendish challenges. One I came across invited you to ride a bike on which, by some sleight of hand, the front wheel turned in the opposite direction to the handlebars. There was a prize for those who could stay on. Few could for it was surprisingly difficult

All the organisers of these events did their very best to provide a colourful show and well-stocked stalls, but the best I remember was at Prestbury – where else? Lots of bunting, lots of very smart people, lots of quite high-pressure salesmanship to support this stall or that. Oh, and invariably lots of sunshine.

Perhaps the most appealing of these affairs were the ones that incorporated the crowning of a queen. Fanshawe Fete is of course famous for its Water Lily Queen who glides over Redesmere in a make-believe swan, and other villages still have their rose queens. But in days gone by there were queens by the score. Almost every church had one, and the crowning was the signal for pageantry and splendour on a touching scale. This is where the silk industry proved a decisive advantage. The queen, her attendants and possibly page boys as well all had to be dressed in a finery becoming the occasion. Almost every member of the committee then knew someone who could obtain the choicest fabric, or sew the neatest of hems. or embroider the most elegant of stitches. The result moved bystanders to rapture as the queen, sometimes just a young girl trying hard to walk regally, led the procession wearing shining silk or satin and a proud smile. She was flanked by attendants with their baskets of flowers, and accompanied also by anxious mothers ready for any little disaster.

To be honest, you didn't even need a queen to put on this style. Choir festivals and flower festivals – these were frequent events in summer, and all called for the young girls to wear white dresses and carry flowers. Some stamina was necessary, since churches and chapels joined forces for these events. Thus Church Street West chapel, with which I had some connection since my great aunt and uncle were caretakers, 'twinned' with Park Green chapel. This was fine for the Church Street West contingent, who happily skipped down Mill Street in their best; it was not so good for the Park Green congregation when, in their turn, they had to climb the hill in the opposite direction. But still, what was that effort when Methodists were quite happy, I was assured, to walk out to Over Alderley chapel for a Sunday evening service?

My turn came during the war when Henbury church held its own choir sermons, starting from its twin centre of Broken Cross. Not only did the choir have to march in their robes, but the big brass cross had to be carried at the head of the parade for the full half-mile. I was proud enough to do this duty when it was only a matter of walking down the aisle; on this occasion the cross was passed from boy to boy as if it was the baton in a relay race.

The South Park bandstand in its days of sunlit glory. The peak of Shutlingsloe is just visible on the right.

None of these activities, which so brightened our summer days, would hold much appeal for today's young generation who are used to heading for Antigua or the Canaries, with or without a cross. But for so many people this was all that there was, and they were grateful.

There were winter fetes too, but of course these had a different atmosphere. In the month before Christmas there were so many events that the *Times* and *Courier* journalists had to share their reports because we couldn't get round to every one on our own. In those happy days of saturation coverage every fete had to be attended and every stallholder mentioned – if some were inadvertently left out, they went in the following week as a correction. Mount Tabor again comes to mind; I recall trekking wearily round each stall and sideshow there, writing down names of the helpers and names of the winners. There were some curious rules. Because of the law on lotteries we were not supposed to name the winners of raffles – they were referred to as special prizes. And in the Santa Season we could never say that John Smith played the part of Father Christmas – what would the young readers have thought? We had to say that John Smith played 'an important role'.

Naturally, it didn't always need the organisation of adults to provide us with jolly days when we were lads. A trip to the park offered great fun at practically no expense whatsoever. In West Park we climbed the great glacier stone (when there was no parkie about to stop us), ogled the mummy in the museum, and watched the birds flying in the aviary attached to the house by the Prestbury Road gate. Even if it rained we didn't care – we could sit in the dinky little wooden octagonal shelters and swap stories. At South Park, for a very modest cost, we played very modest tennis on the hard courts, and larked happily on swings and roundabouts. At Victoria Park, with the bowling green next to the road, we watched the players and tried to work out why the bowls curled in at the end of their run.

At all the parks, naturally, we kept off the grass as instructed. Such a law-abiding lot we were. What would the old-time park attendants say now when young people can't even keep off the flowerbeds?

If time was short we didn't even have to get into town to find our occupations. The Broken Cross recreation ground was on the doorstep, and roughly where the houses of Bromley Road now stand we had an American swing from which to hang upside down, an ocean wave which we tried to rock off its pivot, and a spider's web on which we wobbled to our feet as it whizzed round. Our lasting sorrow was that it didn't boast a crown, the wooden roundabout of which there were specimens in West and South Parks.

Truly, we seemed to have so much to keep us occupied and amused. Perhaps we could think of only one thing to make our happiness complete: what would we have given to find a boat or two on the South Park lake? To boys who had pulled a nifty oar on the North Shore boating pool in Blackpool it was a great deprivation to see an expanse of water and have no means of playing on it.

If all these activities could be enjoyed for almost nothing, some cash was definitely required when the fair came to town twice a year. The mountains of brandy snaps and nougat to which we had been accustomed vanished as the war went on, but there remained the roundabouts – sixpence for the big Waltzer and Speedway rides, twopence or threepence for such pale amusements as the swingboats. However, I have to confess that once, having paid the attendant for a double ride, I had to call him to stop my swingboat as I felt proper queer. The only consolation was that I had slipped off early from school to enjoy this ride so none of my pals was with me to see my green discomfiture. At any rate, one could wander without queasiness round the stalls. I did like the rifle ranges but, of course, there was in the war a shortage of rifles as they had sterner duties to perform. We had to get used to rather cissy occupations like throwing mops at piles of tins, or rolling pennies hoping to win sixpence. But it was all great fun.

So, in a different way in the early forties, was The Day the Circus Came to Town. Whose circus it was I don't remember; what I do recall is the fact that, by means of the bush telegraph, word spread like wildfire that assistance was required in the field where Puss Bank school now stands. We rushed along on our bikes and found a veritable army of young boys. Under the direction of the circus bosses we worked (as it seems to me now) like navvies, hauling on ropes to make the big top big enough. After all this we were invited to return later in the day and, at greatly reduced prices on account of our efforts, watch

Peter Forbes Robinson, who went on to become a famous operatic bass, congratulates his brother Roy and the bride, Jean Powell, after their wedding at St George's Church, Macclesfield, in 1954. Roy was then deputy organist at St George's under Edgar Gulliford, and was later the organist at Christ Church before returning to St George's as organist. The bridesmaid was Margaret Carter.

the show. By this time I had heard of the great tightrope walker, Blondin, who carried a man on his shoulders over Niagara Falls; this circus boasted a high-wire artiste named Blondini and, while that final 'i' made a lot of difference, we were still impressed by his daring.

Some of our days were happy and memorable because of visits by people we had admired from afar. John Mills and Patricia Roc, for example, came to town to shoot scenes for the 1947 film of James Hilton's novel, So Well Remembered. Many local people appeared as extras; I was told the casting office was in W Dewhurst's yard in Jordangate, but I was too shy to approach it.

Then there was the great Wilfred Pickles who, with Mabel, brought their radio team to the Town Hall and broadcast an episode of 'Have a go!'

But the greatest of these days was the visit in 1950 of Princess Elizabeth and the Duke of Edinburgh. Everyone wanted to see them, and schoolchildren were ushered to vantage points by their teachers. Other reporters covered the interesting parts of the visit, like the speeches or factory tours; my duty on that day was to write a description of the enthusiasm with which the crowds in Park Green greeted the royal car as it drove by in stately fashion, and finally to join the little knot of townspeople who waved goodbye outside the Setter Dog as the couple drove away up Buxton Road heading for Chatsworth.

For most families one day shone out above all others as the happiest – a wedding day. Tidily planned, modestly ambitious, carefully supervised by the bride's mother – it didn't require too much to make everyone happy and content. I speak as something of an expert on these matters. For one thing, I played the organ for the first time at a wedding when I was 11 – a neighbour's daughter was getting married and, as it was wartime, there was no other organist around. So there I perched, up in the balcony having my first view of the ceremony while Geoff Bayley pumped away at the bellows. But I came to have wide-ranging knowledge of these things through my role at the *Macclesfield Times*.

Despite the sort of misadventure I have described, when I put in an account of a wedding that hadn't then taken place, I turned out wedding reports by the hundred, based on the answers to questions on the forms. The bride's dress? I became quite an expert on the subject of grosgrain and figured satin. The difference between matrons of honour and bridesmaids and attendants was quite clear to me. I even learned to respect the shyness of couples who insisted that their honeymoon would be spent 'at an undisclosed destination' – often it meant they were decorating the cottage they were renting, and certainly no one would have thought they were going to the Bahamas. There was, however, no question relating to the bridegroom's attire. Unlike today, it was taken for granted that he would be wearing a dark and sober suit with, at the least, a collar and tie.

The forms which yielded up all this vital information winged their way to the bride's family as a result of our close intelligence operation. It would not do to find that we had missed a wedding, and so anyone who could have any possible hand in a marriage ceremony was visited weekly by one of the reporters, in the same way as we checked on all the undertakers. Who would know about forthcoming weddings? Vergers of the churches, of course, so we asked them, and among others I called weekly upon Mr Mitchell of St George's. Owners of the cars who would take the bridal party to church? Of course, so someone was earmarked to make inquiries of the Co-op and of Moss and Smith, who had that curiously isolated garage at the top of the car park at the end of Great King Street.

Cafes where receptions would be held were also questioned. I have already referred to the Macclesfield Arms and the UCP at different ends of the scale, but in between there were some excellent restaurants. The Co-op had their Beehive Cafe in Sunderland Street, very nicely panelled in oak and scene of many a pleasant reception including mine. The Savoy over Burton's came rather late into the picture, but it was here that, on a Wednesday and therefore press night I caught up breathlessly with a wedding that nearly escaped the net. No form for this Wednesday ceremony had been returned, but at my earnest request, standing at the top of the stairs and speaking through one of the guests inside, I persuaded the bride's mother to abandon her ham salad and come and give me all the information. At another wedding, and in desperation, I actually handed a form to the bridegroom as he sat in his front pew awaiting the bride. These things have to be done when the presses are waiting.

Also playing a big part were the suppliers of flowers. I have fond recollections of Cissie Dorey who worked in her family fruit, flower and veg shop in Old Park Lane and turned out masses of bouquets and in due season – despite bleeding fingers – hundreds of holly wreaths as well. Her charges which seemed modest at the time, now appear grotesquely so; a bridal bouquet cost £3.10s, and 15 buttonholes for the men totalled £2.5s.

Weddings are above all else activities guided by strict etiquette. I learned this when we got to hear of the forthcoming wedding of a young lady at Sutton whose family were judged just a bit too important for a stereotyped form. The editor decided that a personal interview was called for, and in a moment of weakness sent me. As soon as the bride's mother opened the door I could see she was a bit nervous. Yes, she would let me interview the bride but she insisted that she must sit in on the exchange. I ploughed on with my questions but I realised I was making my first personal acquaintance with a phenomenon I had encountered previously only in novels – the chaperone. I should have told the mother that, young as I looked, I was a happily married man myself.

In the years that have followed, and in the course of my new duties, I have come to have an even closer acquaintance with the niceties and the pitfalls of weddings. It would not really do to mention any of these except, perhaps, one that stands for me as an Awful Warning of what can occur. In the early days of conducting weddings I was blessing the ring, which rested on my prayer book, when to my horror, as if by magic, it began to slide downwards. I watched, unable to move, as it gathered pace and finally shot off the edge like Eddie the Eagle in an Olympic ski jump. I looked in terror at a nearby central heating grating ... but the bride, Diane, keeping a cool head, bless her, spotted the ring resting in a piece of embroidery on her dress, and handed it back. I pretended these things happened every week.

Ah, happy days! Happy, happy days.

20

Hard Times Come Again No More

It would be hopelessly naive, and insulting to the efforts of Macclesfield people who struggled so hard to make the best of things, to suggest that life in the old town was golden all the time for some, or even a bit of the time for everyone. A sheltered upbringing I may have had, but there was no hiding from even a small boy the facts of poverty and illness and despair. It seems only just that I should mention some of these things, if only in one short chapter, to pay a tribute to the courage and the tenacity that so many people showed in days gone by.

While I was growing up in my two-child family there were others in the town with ten or more children, all in one cottage. They slept as many as four or five to a bed, head to foot, and sometimes conditions must have been indescribable. That they survived at all was due to the long labour of the father who brought home scanty wages, the grinding toil of the mother, and the efforts of the older children who in turn, and from the age of four upwards, had to do their bit to care for the youngest. They had also to earn the odd bob or two when they could to eke out the family income. For very little wage errand boys were sent off on long, tiring and quite paltry delivery journeys on their bikes; to Prestbury, for example, with just four loaves.

While my mother was working at the office she had, during the war, a little friend, a girl of six or seven, who lived in a cottage down the hill in Lower Exchange Street, and who used to call in regularly at the *Times*. She came for a warm by the fire, a biscuit or cake if there was one to spare, and for a chat. She was never cheeky or demanding; she took what was offered with gratitude. She came for two or three years, and then passed out of our lives, and I often wondered what happened to her and the hundreds like her in cottages lining the streets, and in cottages packed into the courts behind the streets. Most moving of all, as I remember, is the fact that the difficulties and the sorrows of life at home were not spoken about to us. It was not the done thing to parade them in front of strangers. If life was hard you got on with it as best you could without much in the way of help, except from the family and kindly neigh- bours. But when it came it was appreciated. My father's family remembered their grandmother saying 'God bless Lloyd George' whenever she went off to collect the five-shillings-a-week old age pension which he had introduced.

Just how tight people's budgets could be was brought home to me when, at six or seven, I spied a toy fort in Harold Wright's shop window in Chestergate, and desired it. The price was 4s 6d, say 23 new pence. I mentioned it not to my family but to Mrs Watkin, relying upon her kindness to do something about it. After much thought she replied that all she could do was, in the words of a radio programme at the time, to 'put a penny on the drum', and see if others could do the same. With the carelessness of youth I thought this a bit mean. But then, as I have mentioned, 4s 6d could pay the rent of your home for a week, or pay the week's food bill.

Through all this struggle there was a fierce determination to live as independently and as quietly as possible. Take, for example, the matter of funerals. These were the days when, as part of a universal recognition that those who had come to their journey's end deserved a final tribute, people stood in silence on the edge of the pavement as a cortege drove by, and the men without exception doffed their caps in respect. This didn't prevent a certain wryness. Part of the folklore handed down in Sheila's family concerned the funeral of an aged relative at which one of the younger mourners, surveying the bent and frail contemporaries gathered round the grave, was heard to observe: 'It's a pity to send some of them home'.

With all the poverty about, then, it was a wonder that people were still concerned about having as good a send-off as possible. Why worry about these things which will be someone else's problem when you have gone? But that was not the thinking, even of the poorest. Grave spaces might be sold according to class, first or second, just as churches had front or back pews depending on how much you could pay, but still you did the best you could. Penny burial clubs were desirable and popular. It seems ridiculous now to contemplate being buried on the proceeds of a penny a week, but it worked then. Respectable parents, anxious to do what was right, signed up their children as soon as they were born, a penny a week was handed over for perhaps 60 or even 70 years, and at the end (with interest) there was around £20 or £25 which, before the war, would see to your 'arrangements'. After all, a grave in the cemetery cost only £3.

Even just after the war the system still held good, because a funeral then could be had for around £25 if you didn't insist on more than one car for the mourners. By that time I knew something of the undertakers who strove to meet the quite modest expectations of bereaved families. To make sure that no interment escaped a mention in the *Times* each reporter had on his list his share of the undertakers, and they had to be visited weekly to see what funerals they were conducting. The 'big three' in those days were Joe Lowe of Sunderland Street (soon to become the Co-op under Frederick Savage) whose shop window always displayed a tasteful stone vase; George Hooley of James Street, always solemn and upright; and Wadsworth's in Beech Lane. These

Dear departed days . . . a horse-drawn hearse outside the undertaking premises of J T Wadsworth, then in a cobbled Jordangate

were attended to by the senior reporters, but there were then several other undertakers in the town, and my beat was among them.

I called on Mr Mellor in Chapel Street, Mr Holland at Broken Cross (once leaving his name off the bottom of my report, to his great sorrow since it was an advert for him), and Mr Greenwood, of Chatham Street. He operated from what I remember as quite a small cottage and didn't have a funeral too often. But as soon as he opened the door to me I knew if he had one that week, because his face glowed with quiet satisfaction. I know this may sound callous, but after all he too had his precarious living to earn.

Despite all the craving among families to live respectably, subterfuge had sometimes to be used to get through the week. A popular stratagem, I am assured, concerned the rent man. Before the war, when it was not thought necessary to lock your front door and callers could drop into your home to transact their business while you were out, it was common for working wives to leave their rent book and rent on the windowsill inside, where it was visible. But should there be no money for the rent that week, the next best thing was to leave the rent book where the rent man could see it but lock the door. This action, it was thought, convinced the landlord you were willing to pay, but were just absent-minded in fastening the door behind you.

Still, this was evidence that people were trying, on their own, to surmount their difficulties. There was no DSS to turn to, and of course no credit cards to manipulate. The sheer battle to survive was sometimes pitiful to see. In the great winter of 1947, when I was old enough to take more notice of these things, I saw the lines of children and adults, waiting at the gasworks for coke which might give them some warmth at home. They filled up buckets and bags and old prams with the stuff, and then had to get it home, struggling up Hibel Road or Buxton Road or Queen Victoria Street. It was either that, or freeze.

I suppose it was scenes like this, repeated of course all over the country, which had been responsible at the end of the war for a quiet revolution, a feeling that things could and should be better, and there was a great ground-swell for change which of course resulted in a Labour landslide in the 1945 election. I was then a schoolboy, but the choices before the country gripped me and millions of others with a fervour which I have never detected since in politics. We used to cut lunch so that we could rush down to Waters Green where, I recall, we heard the speeches of H Fraser Urquhart, the Labour candidate who was opposing Air Commodore A V Harvey (Conservative) and E A B Fletcher (Liberal). Macclesfield held firm for Conservatives – but only just, when you think of today's big majorities. The result declared in August was: Harvey 23, 495, Urquhart 20,442, Fletcher 7,702; majority 3,053.

All this talk of struggle and sorrow and poverty may sound rather vague and far away, but I offer you two genuine stories, still quite clear in my memory through their simple tragedy, though the events happened 55 years ago.

I should say first that, as I remember things from those days, strong efforts were made to keep the facts of death from young people. On the night my Grandfather Maybury died in Christie's my mother returned from his bedside and straightaway supervised rehearsals for a pantomime we were presenting in Henbury school. Only afterwards did she tell us what had happened, and we didn't go to the funeral.

But, the thing was there before our eyes. However well-meaning older relatives were, youngsters came face-to-face with great sorrows and without being told reached an understanding of the tragedies people faced. These are the two that I recall.

First, there were Mrs Watkin's neighbours in Lyon Street, an old couple named Newall. They were kindly folk, if a little baffled by the ways of a young boy. On the odd occasions when Mrs Watkin couldn't get our meal, the Newalls stepped in to provide it. They did their best, even if they did try to persuade me to have a spoonful of jam in my rice pudding which I thought (and still think) a repellent habit.

One night Mr Newall was taken ill. Mrs Watkin was alerted to crisis by a time-honoured signal – Mrs Newall rattled a poker in the grate. But despite the help of neighbours the old man died, and I was taken to see his widow. What I remember is a sense not only of loss after many years of marriage, but of desolation – what could the future hold for a woman alone, without the help of a partner?

The second episode touched me even more deeply. In a tiny bungalow near our home in Henbury lived another old couple, Mr and Mrs Carter, who always seemed pleased to see us when we called in, and chatted away most happily. But Mr Carter became ill. I heard mentioned – without understanding it – the terrible word, 'senility'. One day we were told that Mr Carter was to be taken away to Arclid hospital, a journey of 12 miles. Mrs Carter had no transport of her own. If she could get into town she could catch the Crewe bus, and face a journey of three-quarters of an hour. But she was old herself. When I saw her I found her trying to display a dignified sorrow, but deeply distressed. It was plain that her husband would not come home again; it was possible that she would not be able to go and see him again. She knew it was the end.

Tragedies like these, of course, still happen today. Perhaps I recall these old ones so keenly because they sprang upon me unawares, as it were, when kindly grown-ups were trying to pretend they didn't happen. And they sowed within me the seed of a very great feeling for all of us on this pilgrimage, a prayer which Stephen Foster called the song and the sigh of the weary: 'Hard times, hard times, come again no more'.

21

Gone But Not Forgotten

It can't really come as any surprise that the passing of 60 and more years has brought changes in a living, growing and busy town. There are bound to be regrets that buildings and institutions which were familiar have been altered or vanished altogether, but needs change, and people and their customs change, and allowance has to be made for that. However, while we stride forward to meet the next challenge no one is likely to resist a backward glance in homage to the past and to provide some guidelines for the future. There are lessons we can learn, though sometimes all we can do is acknowledge that change could not be avoided.

What could the mills have done, for example, when new materials and new sources of supply from overseas and new techniques came to dominate the market? Not a great deal, as it turned out. So one by one, with a stealth that misled so many watchers into thinking that the latest closure must be the last, the great mills fell and one morning we awoke to find that almost everything had gone, and whatever we were or could become we were no longer the silk town we had been.

The vast citadel that was BWA, its complex spread over Fence Avenue and the bottom end of Hurdsfield, took some time to lose its identity altogether, its final outpost closing only in the last couple of years. This was the series of mills where my Grandpa Maybury toiled so long and so hard. He should have retired in the war but, like very many others, realised he must carry on with vital work 'until the lads came home again'. Alas, he never made it. How could he or anyone else have foreseen the decline that was to come? But now other companies plus a pub and shops have moved on to the site where BWA's great mills stood, with their spinning rooms and weaving sheds, though the name of the old giant still survives as part of the firm of Bodycote International.

The desolation of the lower end of Hurdsfield, caused by the withdrawal of BWA, was compounded by the obliteration (there is no other word for it) of the adjoining little township that was centred on Commercial Road. Here there were 30 to 40 more or less thriving shops, seven or eight pubs, a school and mission hall and Methodist church, the Beaconsfield Club (named after the great Disraeli and meant to serve working class Conservatives), and some hundreds of small but much-loved houses in Arbourhey Street, Daybrook Street, Fence Street, Waterloo Street and others. All of these were swept aside to make way for the Victoria Flats, one of the most amazing attempts at postwar housing (I choose my words carefully) that I have seen. I wonder if the townspeople thought they had a fair exchange?

Anyway, back to the mills – if only we could. Another of the great enclaves literally to fall was that of G H Heath and Co, whose premises fronted Pickford Street but spread north to encompass Lower Exchange Street and Boden Street. No trace of these mills remain, and the site is now given over to the Discount Giant supermarket and a furniture and electrical store. The great Neckwear complex, which stood on both sides of King Edward Street and had its offices in Henderson Street, has suffered a dismal fate – the land is now a car park. The Depot Mill at the foot of Mill Street has become offices and a bank, while the famous Frosts Mill is given over to the highly successful Gradus enterprise. The company also took over the adjoining building which was Park Green Chapel, then in the war became the British Restaurant which closed on August 18 1945, its job of feeding the hungry town having been accomplished.

The large, plain and squat mill in St George's Street, which housed various firms including Hewetsons and the family firm of Arnold's, which has only just closed, has gone to make way for a row of town houses, while Hewetsons main Albion Mill in London Road still stands but now has a variety of occupants in various trades.

It is not only the silk mills that have perished. The giant Hovis mill at the top of Brook Street, shrine to the particular brand of brown bread which was launched in the town and fed half the world with buttered toast, awaits a new future. There are plans to turn it into flats.

Another empire that disappeared with a suddenness every bit as amazing as the mills was that of the Macclesfield Equitable Provident Society – to you and me, the Co-op or stores. Its main premises, as you see from the picture, used to be in Sunderland Street, but by the time I came to know it there was a new and imposing building in Park Green. This embraced a clothing, materials and haberdashery store on three floors, a pharmacy and shoe shop with, through the door and up the substantial stairs, the offices and a bank. This was the domain of Mr Martin and his management team and also the home of the Co-op's telephone exchange (Macclesfield 3171 and six lines) which was under the command of Joan Barber.

This handsome building is now home to a bed shop, tile shop, wine bar, and the county and magistrates' courts. The original row of Co-op shops in Sunderland Street became the furniture and menswear departments (this building is now demolished), and lower down the street was the Co-op fruit and veg shop (now unoccupied). Opposite was the great Beehive cafe (now the Jubilee Chinese restaurant), while the cake shop and butcher's beneath have become the premises of a bedroom furniture store. There was also a

The Co-op's central premises in Sunderland Street before the Park Green headquarters were built. This row of shops later housed the furniture and men's tailoring departments, among others, but is now demolished.

Co-op cake shop at the bottom end of Chestergate, but its site is now marked by a very swish metal archway with clock.

Dearer to the hearts of the ordinary shopper were the 20 or so neighbourhood grocery stores run by the Co-op. Here there was the excitement not only of watching your grocery parcel tied up with string but also the worry of remembering your Co-op number (12426 in my case). This was written on one of a sheet of little pink receipts with indelible pencil. I still remember the taste of these pencils as you wet them on your tongue; what must they have done to the tongues of the counter staff and the branch managers like Ada Foxwell, one of many good and loyal servants of the Co-op? Anyway, the idea was to provide about six copies of this one receipt – one for you, the rest so that your 'divi' could be reckoned up by the office staff. If your family were wise they also kept a check on their own receipts and did their own totting up; at 2s 10d divi for every pound spent

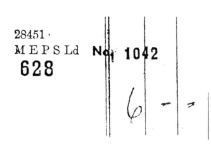

Remember the little pink Co-op checks, written out for you in indelible pencil?

it was worth having all you were entitled to.

Many of these individual shops were most attractive in their day, being built with a family likeness in red brick with cream stone. I'm sure you remember yours – but they have all either vanished or are put to new use. This is my list: Commercial Road (gone), Chester Road (now a Helping Hand store of aids for the disabled), Brown Street (Bayley's electrical store), Jordangate (now offices and unrecognisable as a shop), Bank Street (gone), Cross Street (now a three-piece suite emporium), Crompton Road (empty shop), Roe Street (swept away by the new road), Lower Buxton Road (heating engineers), Higher Buxton Road (door and worktop store), Park Lane (motor accessories), Hurdsfield Road (plant hire), Broken Cross grocery and butchery (empty shops), London Road (now a Late Shop), and John Street (now Dale's oatcake bakery). I'm glad about that last, since oatcakes are among my favourite dishes and it gives me the chance to sing their praises.

Mention of Joan Barber at the Co-op telephone switchboard reminds me of the main GPO switchboard over the old Post Office in Castle Street. I was able to visit it once or twice, and marvelled at the dexterity and the nimble-mindedness of the operators – mostly young ladies – as they worked their lines and plugs like knitting to put through trunk calls to all locations from Manchester to Machynlleth. Now that we can all dial Timbuktu direct, of course, there is no need for a Macclesfield exchange, and all the operators and supervisors like May Pass and Mary Naden have departed from the scene.

Very many individual shops have vanished, of course, in these years, and especially notable are the town centre food shops which had to bow the knee to the supermarkets. There were the old-fashioned grocers, full of lovely smells and with opened tins of biscuits placed temptingly to hand. Many of the managers, like Wilf Renshaw at Burdin's, had a soft spot for youngsters and doled out a chocolate biscuit or two when mum wasn't looking. Nearby rivals to Burdin's in Mill Street were Burgon's, the Home and Colonial, Pegram's and the Maypole, with Seymour Mead's lording it over the Market Place.

Among the smaller shops, who remembers the clogger's in Cross Street, next to Pickford's fruit and veg shop which is itself one of the town's great survivors? Then there was Ray's sport shop in Mill Street whose owner had unfortunately little to sell in the war. I once went there hoping to buy a cricket scorebook for the use of our aero club team, but finding he had none in I settled for a badminton scorebook. It seemed a poor exchange. Another of my haunts was a sweetshop at the corner of Pierce Street and Great Queen Street where with our ha'pennies we played a game that involved sticking a skewer into one of many holes on a board. This (if it was your day) released a little ball which won you a lucky bag or a bigger prize, depending on the ball's colour.

I also recall not only vanished shops but vanished varieties of chocolate; I bought a Double Six chocolate bar with mixed fruit cream filling at a tiny shop in Brown Street, and the original flatter (and better) Aero bar at a shop in Chester Road just past the Regency Mill. Fry's Five Boys bars and many of the shops that sold them have also gone.

Even worse, quite apart from the Commercial Road debacle, some more whole streets have vanished, let alone shops. Derby Street is a noted casualty, since it included not only the Salvation Army Hostel and Atlas printing works but also the white-tiled V E Friedland's plastics factory and an enchantingly old-fashioned store where I bought (for a very poor bonfire night) some Bengal matches. The northern end of Derby Street, from its junction with Great King Street to Chestergate, used to contain Ashton's sports shop, Avery scales and the Gospel Hall of blessed memory. This section still has a vicarious sort of existence somewhere under Churchill Way, but the lower end has vanished altogether. Where it used to debouch into Mill Street, flanked by New Day furniture shop on one corner and the Cable shoe shop on the other, there is now an impenetrable line of big stores. The line of Derby Street must pass behind the Cheshire Building Society and be buried beneath the new Post Office. In the same area, Thomas Street and the wryly named Prospect Buildings have also departed.

On the other side of town there has been quite a grand clearance and rebuilding of houses around Bank Street, with its satellites Jodrell Street and Knight Street among others. Some of the space thus liberated is occupied now by Winlowe, sheltered housing for the elderly named very touchingly after a much respected housing manager in the town. Around it are many new maisonettes and houses with gardens, which few of the older homes possessed.

Then there were the streets of houses that used to stand behind the Majestic – Silk and Cotton Streets, Charles Street, and Barker Street which led down to the Dam Steps (we weren't supposed to say those words when we were young). A little bit of this area was used as a car park by those few Majestic patrons who actually motored to the pictures; now the whole site is a car park.

Also vanished from this area is Duke Street school, where my two aunts were educated, and which looked such an impressive building on its eminence above Samuel Street. Mill Street school (actually in Lower Exchange Street) has also gone, but what is claimed to be the original doorstep is still visible on the right of the street as you go down, just before coming to the furniture store. So that may be a little bit of history you can actually touch.

Both these were church schools – Mill Street was Methodist and Duke Street C of E. Of the other church schools St George's and St Peter's have been converted into flats, along with Brunswick schoolroom. St George's, incidentally, was Sheila's old primary school, and it lives on in our household through

Two casualties for the price of one – this tranquil old picture of West Park shows the spire of Trinity Methodist Church (where Mr Southwell and I both played the organ in our different ways) and the infirmary on the left. Both these buildings have been demolished.

the name of one of the teachers, Miss Earles. She read a story a day to the youngsters, asked at the end how they had liked it, and they were supposed to say: 'Very nice, Miss Earles'. This phrase has now become a term of the warmest approbation in the Maybury family.

The town's churches themselves have also suffered greatly at the hands of Father Time. Closures began before the war, but in the last forty and fifty years they have continued at breakneck pace and especially, unfortunately, among the Methodist buildings. There were still a dozen of them in the 1950s, but how have they fared?

The great Wesley's Chapel in Sunderland Street – where Mr Somerscales the minister and I as a reporter were once the only men among a congregation of 200 women – is now a snooker club. Brunswick, which was built at the same time as St George's so that locals seeing them go up together called them St George and the Dragon, that is now empty awaiting a new use, although the great organ has been saved. Trinity, where Mr Southwell and I both played the organ in our different ways, was demolished along with its impressive spire, and Trinity old people's home now stands on the site. Park Lane chapel, which once echoed to the sound of those glorious concerts, rings now to the sound of Harvest Printers machinery. Stamford Road chapel on the Moss, which I remember scrubbed and polished and shining brightly on a Daffodil Day in the forties, has been turned into flats. Bourne Chapel in Byron Street, Mount Tabor off Windmill Street and Fence Chapel in Waterloo Street have vanished. Church Street West has become offices, but its former incarnation is still obvious to those who study the building.

Beech Lane and South Park Road Methodist churches have soldiered on, but now there are plans to build one town centre church in King Edward Street to replace them. That might leave Broken Cross Church, scene of many of our boyhood exploits, as the only other Methodist survivor in the town.

Nor have Church of England churches been immune from change. St John's in Statham Street was demolished and replaced by a new church on the Weston estate. This was built in the modern style, with a roof meant to look like a fish, but unfortunately to the local lads it looked like a skateboarding ramp. There was continual trouble with its weatherproofing and eventually, in 1994 that too was demolished and a third church built. The biggest casualty for Anglican congregations, however, has been the closure of the great Christ Church, built in 1775 by the local magnate Charles Roe with a tower which aimed to be equal in height to that of the Parish Church, and in whose great pulpit John Wesley himself often preached. Much effort is being spent on renovating the church; its grounds, after some years of neglect, have already been restored and surrounded by smart new walls and railings.

The Salvation Army has moved from its citadel in Mill Street, whose antecedents as the Theatre Royal were still obvious to visitors, and their headquarters are now in the former Parochial Hall in Roe Street. The Town Mission, whose homely meeting place in Mill Street was much loved by a devoted band of elderly ladies, was well served in his day by Mr Pybus, while one of his successors, Pastor Sutton, is remembered for the gifts of tinned food he took to the folk on whom he called. But the meeting place itself became a health studio and then a snooker club, and the Town Mission changed to the Christian Mission dedicated under Stuart George to serving all the town's places of worship.

With Christians in mind we should also perhaps mourn the passing of the YWCA premises which stood at the bottom end of Jordangate. Here on press nights the younger members of the *Times* and *Courier* editorial staffs would meet for a tea of cheese on toast, and perhaps a game of table tennis on a table squashed into one of the rooms above. Along with Evans the newsagent's and several cottages the YWCA was demolished, and a new multi-storey car park has arisen on their site.

From churches we can turn to a building which had the proportions of a cathedral – but which, alas, was dirtier and smellier. This was the gasworks which dominated Gas Road (naturally) and the bottom end of Hibel Road where it swept sharply to the right and could be taken at a good belt by the motorcyclist. The gasworks was always worth a visit to a boy with time on his hands for it incorporated an interesting device which emptied coal trucks in the railway sidings and delivered their contents up a steep and covered escalator to the gasworks on the other side of the road. From a wall under the railway bridge just up the road a good view could also be had of the Bollin as it slid moodily along its twilit culvert towards the green fields of its dreams.

From gas it's only a short step to petrol, and the garages that served us with the stuff. Most of them then had old-fashioned pumps (some hand-operated) on the inside of the pavement, with the hose snaking up round a swinging arm which took it to the roadside and your petrol tank. Mr Simcock had a couple of these pumps at Broken Cross, and there were more at Cookson's in Waters Green (plus their little satellite filling station in Beech Lane), Ford and Challinor in Chestergate (which also put on show a few toys at Christmas) and Stanways in Great King Street. Some, seeing me ride up on my two-stroke motorbike, insisted on mixing the necessary oil and petrol in a can before pouring it into the tank – not bad service when I was buying no more than a shilling's worth.

Now that we're talking about transport we can turn to the stations and the two that Macclesfield has lost. I know that we have the new station in the Waters, but its rather stark concrete outlines are in poor contrast to the mellow, warm-looking brick of the old Central Station where we punched so many

This printed silk picture, one of the famous series produced by Brocklehurst Fabrics Limited over 50 years, captures the atmosphere of power in the now-demolished Hibel Road station. It will also bring back memories of the bookstall at the far end and the long platform where the crowds massed for Barnby trains. In the background looms the cathedral-sized structure of the gasworks. The original picture is, of course, in full colour.

name-plates on the penny slot-machines. There is no doubt, however, that Hibel Road has vanished, and with it the chance to go whooping and shouting down its covered approach, testing the echoes and the patience of the station staff.

It was great fun, and helped to while away the hours of waiting for wartime trains, to stand at the north end of the platform from where you could see the signalman labouring in his box. The challenge with other boys was to try to work out just what was happening when the bells ting-a-linged and the railman pulled his levers. If we were lucky, the signal on our line turned with a clank from red to green, and we knew our train (at any rate, some train) was on its way. Round about the station were vast sidings and coalyards, and offices to which you had to resort if you were expecting a large parcel. Now there is Tesco and its carpark. But if you peer over the railings in Station Street, by the Ford garage, you can still see what remains of Hibel Road and recall the shrills and hisses and the smell of steam, and reawaken old excitements.

Finally, what of the places of amusement and recreation to which we

A rare reminder of the old Broken Cross post office, in the days before the Co-op built their shop next door. Mrs Hannah Fisher took over the post office in 1896, and in the years that followed it sold a wide assortment of goods including (as I remember with gratitude) bandages. And as every boy with buckled wheels will recall, bicycles were also repaired round the back by her son-in-law, Sydney Barber. In 1943 the post office was transferred – but remained in the family – to the shop at the crossroads kept by Hannah's daughter Gladys Warren and her husband Bill, of radio repair fame. Here the post office still remains, though the business has expanded into what used to be the bus shelter next door.

repaired with such joy? Well, the Stanley Hall has vanished under the precinct, and the Brocklehurst Memorial Hall is a car park. The little 'tin tabernacle', a meeting place opposite King's School which was a mission room run by the Parish Church, is now somewhere beneath the big roundabout at the top of Hibel Road. And the Martineau Hall, named after the great Unitarian James Martineau who was a close friend of Mrs Gaskell from nearby Knutsford, is now after a long and honourable life threatened with replacement. Both these smallish halls were well used for events connected with the Youth Festivals in postwar years. The noble Drill Hall, scene of countless bazaars and antique fairs as well as military manoeuvres, is at this date unoccupied following the building of a new Territorial headquarters on Chester Road.

The former District Bank in the Market Place has been well preserved and given a new life as the town library, freeing the old library in Park Green for new duties as the Register Office. Many of us will remember the original library, with its lofty rooms and its hushed tones which even as children we were unwilling to interrupt. The building lost just a little bit of its good looks when the two imposing flights of steps on the corner, from which John Mills spoke to the townspeople in the film of 'So Well Remembered', had to be removed and the main entrance shifted rather furtively round the corner.

Well remembered indeed ! The old library complete with the steps (now vanished) from which John Mills addressed the crowd in the film of James Hilton's novel 'So Well Remembered'. The building - given by the town's enlightened MP David Chadwick in 1876 - is now the register office.

Well, that's four thousand words just to record in this chapter a few of the changes I've seen. I'm quite sure that each of the 40,000 or so residents could make an equally long list of favourite haunts that have vanished. But funnily enough, I bet that if someone came back to the town after 60 years, and was plonked down in the Market Place or the Waters, Park Lane or Mill Street or any one of dozens of other locations, he or she would still say: 'Eh, it may be knocked about a bit – but it's still the Macclesfield I knew'.

22

Ta-ra To You All

It has been a great pleasure setting down these memories, and a challenge to get them into some sort of order instead of letting them rush out pell-mell as they usually do when the brainbox is stirred up. But as I've written I've come to a conclusion I should have known all along, as I'm sure you do. What I realise is that it's not the one big memory that means so much, but the millions of tiny things taken together that guide your way.

I've mentioned many in these chapters, but there were so many more that I don't even have to dip a bucket into the well of remembering; they come running over of their own accord. Like – here we go again – the stalls in the Market Place (where else should they be?) and the women holding out tasters of cheese for you on the end of their long knives. The lights of the Mill Street shops on a winter's evening snaking down the hill like glow-worms on a switchback. The taste of fresh blackberries that brings back instantly the endless hours of innocent summer fun in the fields around Henbury. And talking of fields, the path I used to walk, without any presentiment of what was to come, through the meadows bright with corn that stretched then from Broken Cross to just above the farm with a water pump in Ivy Road. Now of course all those fields have been planted with houses.

But I've saved to the last the clearest, strangest and yet most persistent of all my memories which comes back to me almost every time I drive up Bond Street. I had been sent by Mrs Watkin to get some sausages from the nearest butcher – was this Oldfield's? As I crossed Lyon Street, went down a little patch of wasteland and so to the entry that led to Bond Street I was mulling over one of life's big problems for a boy of seven or so: 'Why are pies made of pork called pork, but those made of beef are meat?' The ways of grown-ups seemed, as always, a little strange. But as I emerged from the entry and turned right for the shop all such matters vanished and time stood still. I saw Bond Street, rising gently towards Park Lane, in the silence of the midday heat. There was not one car to be seen. There were perhaps only two or three people visible in all the long street which, give or take a shop board or two, looks the same now as it did then.

And this is the scene which I hold to be the truest picture of my home town. I realised later that it needs its important buildings and its prominent people – and on the very day I was setting down these last thoughts, and as if to verify what I was writing, my little grandson and I encountered the Mayor of

Macclesfield quite by chance as he fulfilled an engagement in the South Park. But impressed as we were to see Councillor Russell Cutler, with his gold chain and the official car with its MAC number plate, I trust he will understand if I say that while he is the symbolic head of the town its real heart lies in the friendly people in their many houses and the conscientious traders in their small shops, whose lives can be busy but not so frantic that they don't see what's going on around them.

That Bond Street experience captured in a moment a snapshot of a town that is at peace with not too much clamour about events beyond its reach; a place of sense and solidity, of permanence despite change, of good cheer despite the sorrows and the tragedies that must afflict every one of us in our turn.

All in all, a home town to remember with pride, and a home town with depth. I offer my best wishes to all who share it with me and, in the traditional Macclesfield farewell, say: Ta-ra.

A card from Macclesfield sent in 1914; the message read
"We arrived alright and I hope you will not be lonely"

More about Macclesfield . . .

MACCLESFIELD IN PICTURES & POEMS – Dorothy Bentley Smith *(£6.95)*

PORTRAIT OF MACCLESFIELD – Doug Pickford *(£6.95)*

MACCLESFIELD SO WELL REMEMBERED – Doug Pickford *(£6.95)*

MACCLESFIELD, THOSE WERE THE DAYS – Doug Pickford *(£6.95)*

. . . and elsewhere in the North & Midlands

PORTRAIT OF WILMSLOW, Handforth & ALDERLEY EDGE – Ron Lee *(£7.95)*

PORTRAIT OF STOCKPORT – John Creighton *(£6.95)*

PORTRAIT OF MANCHESTER – John Creighton *(£6.95)*

PORTRAIT OF WARRINGTON – Jen Darling *(£6.95)*

JOURNEY THROUGH LANCASHIRE – Kenneth Fields *(£7.95)*

OLD NOTTINGHAMSHIRE REMEMBERED – Keith Taylor *(£7.95)*

TRADITIONAL PUBS OF OLD LANCASHIRE – Peter Barnes *(£7.95)*

Myths, Legends & Folklore:

SHADOWS: A NORTHERN INVESTIGATION OF THE UNKNOWN – Steve Cliffe *(£7.95)*

DARK TALES OF OLD CHESHIRE – Angela Conway *(£6.95)*

CHESHIRE: ITS MAGIC & MYSTERY – Doug Pickford *(£7.95)*

MYTHS AND LEGENDS OF EAST CHESHIRE – Doug Pickford *(£5.95)*

GHOSTS, TRADITIONS & LEGENDS OF LANCASHIRE – Ken Howarth *(£7.95)*

SUPERNATURAL STOCKPORT – Martin Mills *(£5.95)*

STRANGE SOUTH YORKSHIRE – David Clarke *(£6.95)*

CHILLING TRUE TALES OF OLD LANCASHIRE – Keith Johnson *(£7.95)*

Country Walking – Cheshire & The Peak District

EAST CHESHIRE WALKS – Graham Beech *(£5.95)*

WEST CHESHIRE WALKS – Jen Darling *(£5.95)*

PUB WALKS IN CHESHIRE – Jen Darling *(£6.95)*

TEA SHOP WALKS IN CHESHIRE – Clive Price *(£6.95)*

TEA SHOP WALKS IN THE PEAK DISTRICT – Norman & June Buckley *(£6.95)*

PEAKLAND RIVER VALLEY WALKS – Tony Stephens *(£7.95)*

HALF DAY WALKS IN THE PEAK DISTRICT – Alan Bradley *(£6.95)*

RAMBLES AROUND MANCHESTER – Mike Cresswell *(£5.95)*

Country Walking – further afield

PUB WALKS IN THE YORKSHIRE DALES – Clive Price *(£6.95)*

PUB WALKS ON THE NORTH YORK MOORS & COAST – Stephen Rickerby *(£6.95)*

PUB WALKS IN THE YORKSHIRE WOLDS – Tony Whittaker *(£6.95)*

YORKSHIRE: A WALK AROUND MY COUNTY – Tony Whittaker *(£6.95)*

BEST PUB WALKS IN & AROUND SHEFFIELD – Clive Price *(£6.95)*

BEST PUB WALKS IN SOUTH YORKSHIRE – Martin Smith *(£6.95)*

THE LAKELAND SUMMITS – Tim Synge *(£7.95)*

100 LAKE DISTRICT HILL WALKS – Gordon Brown *(£7.95)*

LAKELAND ROCKY RAMBLES: Geology beneath your feet – Brian Lynas *(£7.95)*

FULL DAYS ON THE FELLS: Challenging Walks – Adrian Dixon *(£7.95)*

PUB WALKS IN THE LAKE DISTRICT – Neil Coates *(£6.95)*

YORKSHIRE DALES WALKING: ON THE LEVEL – Norman Buckley *(£6.95)*

LAKELAND WALKING, ON THE LEVEL – Norman Buckley *(£6.95)*

TEA SHOP WALKS IN THE LAKE DISTRICT – Jean Patefield *(£6.95)*

MOSTLY DOWNHILL: LEISURELY WALKS, LAKE DISTRICT – Alan Pears *(£6.95)*

MOSTLY DOWNHILL IN THE PEAK DISTRICT – Clive Price *(£6.95)*
(two volumes, White Peak & Dark Peak)

WALKS IN MYSTERIOUS WALES – Laurence Main *(£7.95)*

RAMBLES IN NORTH WALES – Roger Redfern *(£6.95)*

PUB WALKS IN SNOWDONIA – Laurence Main *(£6.95)*

FIFTY CLASSIC WALKS IN THE PENNINES – Terry Marsh *(£8.95)*

River and Canal Walks

PEAKLAND RIVER VALLEY WALKS – Tony Stephens *(see Country Walking section)*

WATERWAY WALKS AROUND BIRMINGHAM – David Perrott *(£6.95)*

WATERWAY WALKS IN LEICESTERSHIRE & RUTLAND – Paul Biggs *(£6.95)*

NORTH-WEST WATERWAY WALKS: NORTH OF THE MERSEY – Dennis Needham *(£6.95)*

NORTH-WEST WATERWAY WALKS: SOUTH OF THE MERSEY – Guy Lawson *(£6.95)*

NORTH-WEST WATERWAY WALKS: THE MERSEY WATERWAYS – David Parry *(£6.95)*

Cycling . . .

CYCLE UK! The essential guide to leisure cycling – Les Lumsdon *(£9.95)*

OFF-BEAT CYCLING IN THE PEAK DISTRICT – Clive Smith *(£6.95)*

MORE OFF-BEAT CYCLING IN THE PEAK DISTRICT – Clive Smith *(£6.95)*

CYCLING IN THE LAKE DISTRICT – John Wood *(£7.95)*

50 BEST CYCLE RIDES IN CHESHIRE – Graham Beech *(£7.95)*

CYCLING IN NOTTINGHAMSHIRE – Penny & Bill Howe *(£7.95)*

CYCLING IN SCOTLAND & N.E. ENGLAND – Philip Routledge *(£7.95)*

CYCLING IN NORTH WALES – Philip Routledge *(£7.95)*

CYCLING IN & AROUND BIRMINGHAM – Philip Routledge *(£7.95)*

CYCLING IN & AROUND MANCHESTER – Les Lumsdon *(£7.95)*

Sport . . .

RED FEVER: from Rochdale to Rio as 'United' supporters – Steve Donoghue *(£7.95)*

UNITED WE STOOD: unofficial history of the Ferguson years – Richard Kurt *(£6.95)*

DESPATCHES FROM OLD TRAFFORD – Richard Kurt *(£6.95)*

MANCHESTER CITY: Moments to Remember – John Creighton *(£9.95)*

AN A-Z OF MANCHESTER CITY – Dean Hayes *(£6.95)*

GOLF COURSES OF CHESHIRE – Mark Rowlinson *(£9.95)*

- plus many more entertaining and educational books being regularly added to our list. All of our books are available from your local bookshop. In case of difficulty, or to obtain our complete catalogue, please contact:

Sigma Leisure
1 South Oak Lane, Wilmslow, Cheshire SK9 6AR

Phone: 01625 – 531035   Fax: 01625 – 536800

ACCESS and VISA orders welcome – call our friendly sales staff or use our 24 hour Answerphone service! Most orders are despatched on the day we receive your order – you could be enjoying our books in just a couple of days. Please add £2 p&p to all orders.